It's Always on My Mind

It's Always on My Mind

A Guide to Dating

J. John

Authentic

Dedication

I dedicate this book to Michael, Simeon and Benjamin

Contents

Acknowledgements

I would like to acknowledge the invaluable wisdom of my dear friend, Chris Russell. Many thanks to Sarah Doyle for helping me to shape the book – your assistance was invaluable. Thank you to Auriel Schluter for her insights and extensive contribution to the chapter on 'Dead-End Relationships'. Many thanks to Carrie Boren, Edie Gould and Max Manners for their perceptive reading of the manuscript and for their valuable suggestions.

Preface

Revising a book I thought I had finished years ago has been one of the rare instances in my life when the benefits of hindsight have actually had a positive effect. *It's Always on My Mind* has been written because I keep running into the need for it. The majority of us find that issues of love, sex, relationships and their expectations and disappointments frequently occupy our attention.

The gospel is the amazingly good news that while we were sinners Christ died for us. His forgiveness frees us to live by the power of the Holy Spirit, rejoicing in the goodness of God and all his gifts, including the gift of love and sexuality.

What does God want from us? He wants us to live fully and joyfully for him. The joyous truth of God's goodness is to permeate every part of our lives, including our sexuality. In the bitter debates about sexual morality, we sometimes forget that God invented sex. He could have created us to reproduce by binary fission, but he made us male and female, with the capacity to feel exquisite physical pleasure, to long for emotional intimacy and to commit ourselves in stable, enduring relationships.

Many of us live with old scars, inclinations that draw us in wrong directions, or unfulfilled desires. It is comforting to know that Jesus experienced singleness and loneliness. He died on a cross at the age of thirty-three, having known for a long time that his destiny was to die. What did he feel as he held children he was blessing? What did he feel as he met women and knew he would never marry. His was a much harder road than we will ever have to walk. Dietrich Bonhoeffer wrote, 'Remember, it is possible to have a fulfilled life even if there are many unfulfilled desires.' That is a word of hope for those of us who struggle with dating, singleness or a sexual orientation that God says, 'No' to.

I offer these pages praying they will infuse in you faith, hope and love.

At the end of each chapter you will find a 'Take It Further' section which will help you to think through the issues raised in the chapter and to take appropriate action.

J. John

Chapter 1

For Love's Sake

'Love' is the most frequently written-about subject. Love stories, love poetry, guidebooks to love and love songs have continued since people first put stick to clay. Today, we see love strewn across the media; it is manufactured to advertise almost anything, from perfume to coffee. It has become almost an image accessory. 'Love' is a term we use on so many different levels and yet one struggles to define it.

Love is possible at many levels, but there is a danger of devaluing its currency, of selling it at a discount. It is a tragedy of the times that people have begun to assess love in terms of sexual performance, and when contraception is efficient and available, both men and women are encouraged to let deep urges have their way. For who knows if this time, this latest partner may be the one? And how, without trying this all-important step of sex, can couples know if they are 'in love'? Glamorous and beautiful Hollywood couples declare the depth of their love to the world, yet within months they may be as desperately out of love as they are in love now.

Romantic love is big business. Romantic comedies are

the most popular film genre; they paint perfect and endearing love stories. Boy meets girl; they fall in love, overcoming some kind of obstacle and the film concludes with the couple in a relational bliss which we believe will last forever.

Today in our society it is difficult to talk about love without talking about sex. Sex as nothing but 'recreation' is found in numerous men's magazines. They insist that unmarried sex is the answer to love as long as it is by mutual desire and consent. But in reality, a woman is simply another aspect of the status-symbol mania that is stamped all over the magazines. She is no more or less important than the sleekest sports car or an expensive bottle of wine. A woman becomes depersonalized: an object of a man's pleasure, something to inflate his ego and look gorgeous as he parades her in front of his friends. It is a myth to believe that sex has no personal consequences. The reality is that self-respect and emotional and physical wellbeing are at risk.

Is Love Self-Giving or Selfish?

One of my favourite foods is pizza – I have heard myself say more than once, 'I love pizza' – what do I mean? I love pizza simply for what it does for me. It tastes really good and my appetite is satisfied. Once I have scoffed it down, the pizza no longer fulfils the function, or if I've eaten too much and feel sick, I don't shout out so enthusiastically, 'I love pizza!' My love is not directed to the pizza for itself, but simply to the pizza in so far as it does something for me! The pizza satisfies our hunger temporarily in the same way that passion can sometimes be used to mask our deeper needs.

Sam's party was the talk of the term; Tom had been

looking forward to this for ages. He had battled out a respectable curfew time with his mum and worked out what he was going to wear. The big night arrived.

The evening began well – there were lots of people, all chatting and dancing. Then people began to pair off. Tom felt that old familiar pang of loneliness begin to creep in. He often found he was left on his own. He went to the kitchen to get more cheap drink and soon had too much. In the kitchen was a girl he'd seen at school. He'd not really noticed her before, but now they were thrown together in their loneliness and drunkenness. He suggested they went upstairs and before he knew it they were in the room with all the other couples. He kissed her once, then again. His head was spinning, something was saying, 'Stop!' but he wanted love. He told her he loved her, and before they knew it, they were all over each other – not thinking of how they would face each other on Monday.

Contrast that with the following scenes: New York, September 11, 2001; this date holds harrowing memories for us all. Amidst the trauma and inexplicable devastation lie some tales of outstanding acts of love. The New York Fire Command Centre was situated on the basement floor of the South Tower. When the first tower was hit, the Fire Chief had to make a decision; he decided to remain at this post despite the implicit danger, because this centre had the best facilities available. The Fire Chief and his men worked zealously to try and salvage the lives of others, until the South Tower finally collapsed as well, killing the Fire Chief and the majority of his men.

Consider Mother Teresa, who was born on 27 August 1910 in Skopje, in the former Yugoslavia, of Albanian parents. At the age of eighteen she joined the Congregation of Loreto nuns and for seventeen years taught history and geography in the Loreto High School,

Calcutta. On 10 September 1946, however, came what she described as the 'call within the call'. Her vocation was to leave the convent and step out into some of India's most disease-ridden slums to live as one with the poorest of the poor, and to birth a new community committed wholeheartedly to their service.

I visited Calcutta and saw the Sisters of Charity at work. At one hospice, the smell was sickening and what I saw made me feel weak at the knees and confused in my thoughts. The Sisters of Charity speak loudly, but not with words, to those they seek to help. What is it they say? 'I love you.' Those they were nursing at the hospice were all smiling, despite being in pain and approaching death. They smile, no doubt, only because someone loves them.

Here the love is self-giving and unselfish. The Sisters of Charity look upon the homeless and dying as persons. They do not use them. They simply do what is best for them. They judge that they have value as human beings without any consideration for any service that could be given in return.

> Real love begins where nothing is expected in return.
>   Antoine de Saint Exupery

This attitude, in some way, is true love. True love is fundamentally giving. Despite being a simple concept of love, what it actually means for an individual in practice is not so simple. For one it is giving blood, for another it is giving money to a charity appeal. For someone else it might be giving one's time to a friend who wants to talk about a personal problem. It is often tempting to perform an act of 'giving' purely for a sense of self-gratification. It can make one feel superior, wealthy and powerful, but if the point of giving was to 'feel' these things, did one not give in vain?

The greatest treason is to do the right deed for the wrong reason.

T. S. Eliot

Making others happy attains real happiness. The 'superior-wealthy-powerful' giving, largely for ourselves, is self-centred, and is a symptom of our own inner insecurities. The current philosophy is one of self-assertiveness: 'Seven steps to get what you want', 'How to have time for yourself', 'Learn to say "No"' are just a few of the bold article titles that jump out at us from a newsagent's shelf. Love, however, demands a shift of focus – from an inward to an outward perspective.

There are some basic elements common to all types of love. The first is care and concern for other people. We love someone and that love prompts and motivates in us a positive, active concern for the life and growth of the individual.

A second element common to all types of love is openness. An open person responds to the needs of others. The openness or responsiveness is most easily recognized and met in the physical sense – a poor person needing food or clothing, an accident victim requiring immediate assistance. How closed people can often be can be seen when there is an urgent need of help. A friend of mine recalled an accident that occurred and described how he and his wife, having witnessed the accident from a long way off, ran towards those in need, while many other people, all very near the scene, just stood at the bus stop or looked out of shops and watched! If there is a mugging, people will often walk away because they don't want to get involved, even though someone is being hurt – often we are more concerned for ourselves. We can so easily be all wrapped up in our own little world.

Open love, like all self-giving love, requires effort. We can, of course, close our hearts to these people requesting our help. Some people try to justify themselves, claiming that they just don't want to get too involved. It's a pretty cold, hardened heart that can turn from such severe distress and go about its business apathetically. And if we cannot be open and respond to these needs that can be so easily met, what about the deeper, less obvious needs of others – those inner feelings that can bring more intense pain. Would we have eyes to see and a heart to act? That's what openness is.

The third element is respect. Respect is the ability to see a person as they are, to be aware of their unique individuality. Respect means there is no exploitation. I want the other person to grow and mature for their sake and not what I can get from them.

The fourth basic element of love is understanding. Friends often act or speak in such a way as to inflict real, deep pain. Understanding means not flaring up but having the patience to sense and bring to the surface the root cause of this hurtful activity. If we are the problem, then love enables us to understand quickly. What is important for love and understanding is that we go beneath the surface and prevent a reaction to want to 'hit and hurt back'.

Care and concern for others, openness, respect and understanding are common to all types of love.

Digging Deeper

Our difficulty in defining the word 'love' is due to the English language, where one word covers such a variety of meanings. The early Greeks encountered this difficulty and they produced four different words for love: (i) agape (ii) philia (iii) storge (iv) eros.

Agape means a love that comes from realising and understanding the value and preciousness of a person. It is the love God has for us. God realizes and understands how precious we are. *Agape* means 'selflessness'. *Agape* is a total giving love. This is the love God expressed when he gave his only Son, Jesus Christ, to rescue us from darkness. He had no self-interest. In the human sphere, *agape* love is thoughtfulness, concern and sensitivity to the needs of others.

The Apostle Paul in Ephesians 5:28-29 wrote:

> In this same way, husbands ought to love [agape] their wives as their own bodies. He who loves his wife loves himself. After all, no one ever hated his own body, but he feeds and cares for it, just as Christ does the church.

This love is spelt G-I-V-E. In a giving relationship there is no room for fear, frustration, pressure, envy or jealousy. Mother Teresa was a remarkable example of *agape* love – total giving without expecting anything in return.

The second word is *philia*. *Philia* is friendship, companionship, emotional sharing of time and interests. It is standing beside someone. It is a commitment to someone – knowing their faults and weaknesses, but pledging to stand by their side. A friend is an ally who will give and share when we're in need.

The third word is *storge*. *Storge* means affection, goodwill, concern and kindness. This is the love most often shown to the elderly, to children and to acquaintances and neighbours. It can be a momentary smile or a handshake that is sincere. It doesn't involve physical attraction or desire. It is a love for who the person is and it ignores barriers of age, sex, class or education.

Fourthly, the Greeks use the word *eros*. It is the root of

the word 'erotic'. *Eros* means sexual attraction without the act of sex. It is love that seeks sexual expression – a desire inspired by the biology within humanity. Of itself, *eros* is not wrong, but it should not act on its own. Unfortunately, it is the love that the world would have us believe is the highest kind of love. It is often the only love many people ever experience, but romantic, sensual love is only part of the God-given concept of total love. Let us think carefully when we use the word 'love'.

Take It Further

Bible Study

1 John 3:11–20; 1 John 4:7–12; 1 Corinthians 13.

Talking Points

Think of as many different ways as you can in which the word 'love' is used in our society today. When is it used wrongly? In what ways is it used rightly?

What is unique and different about the love God has shown us through Jesus?

Why and how does God want us to show love to one another?

What is the difference between love that comes from the will and love that comes from the emotion? Try to illustrate this. Can you have one without the other? Does one sometimes lead to the other? What happens when we have both? Which does our society encourage?

For Action

Think of a way you can show *agape* love (i.e. from the will) to someone else. Begin to take note of when love is equated simply with feelings.

God's love involves costly self-giving. Find a new way of giving your time, talents and treasure in a costly way to God's work and others in need.

Chapter 2

Love Yourself

How do people come to love themselves? Or come to hate themselves? At birth a baby does not know whether it is good or bad, lovable or detestable. How is it that we come to know and evaluate ourselves?

Our self-image is largely formed through our relationships. We feel loved or rejected. This begins with parents, then brothers and sisters, grandparents and friends.

When babies are taken care of by their parents or carers, they are cuddled, their nappies changed, attention is given to them when they cry. The baby feels wanted and secure. But when parents are affectionless and don't bother getting up; when the reaction to a baby is frequently irritation or indifference, the baby can feel insecure and fearful.

When the baby becomes a child and is able to understand and communicate with words, not just actions, words from others begin to shape the child's sense of self-worth. This process can cause damage and words leave harmful effects, such as statements like:

'*If* you want your Mum and Dad to really love you, then get an A in your school report.'

'We would love you more *if* you helped around the house.'

'*If* you don't stop doing bad things, then you will never amount to anything and you won't be liked.'

In these statements, love is seen as a reward. A qualified gift to be deserved or earned before it is given. They imply that the child is only loved or is lovable under certain conditions: if they do something, become something, or achieve something. The child's self-esteem can rollercoaster from a high when they feel loved and accepted, then fall to a low when they believe they have disappointed and failed to earn the right to be loved. This is using love as a reward and its withdrawal as a punishment.

Another form of conditional love is when parents – one or both – love children because they need them. If they feel emotionally insecure, they too crave love. The parent, therefore, does everything to gain the child's love and keep them dependent. Some of these children can go through life insisting that they were always loved by their parents and yet at the same time rebelling, feeling unloved and somehow used. Rather than being loved in their own right, they were loved because they filled an emotional need in someone else.

A continuous experience of feeling unloved and therefore not capable of loving oneself can cause frustration, fear and worry. God has put in us an unquenchable desire to be loved and to love. Therefore, feeling unloved takes away joy and peace and replaces them with fear. People are afraid to love and afraid to be loved in case of being rejected and hurt.

God, however, has put in us a healing capacity. When one suffers a wound, blood cells rush to form a healing scar tissue. When there is a fever to destroy an infection, sweat pours out to protect the body from the burning temperature. Similarly, there is a defence and healing mechanism that operates when we are hurt emotionally and psychologically. But, just as sometimes a fever can affect the brain and sweat can cause dehydration, healing of our emotions is not always simple and our defences create complex reactions.

Let us assume that Helen feels she has not been loved unconditionally and therefore feels insecure, unwanted and miserable. She cannot love or accept herself and she strives to achieve in order to gain acceptance and love. In Helen's situation, a number of defences can develop in an attempt to counteract her feelings.

The first is an inferiority complex. Because Helen has never felt loved, she feels inadequate, unworthy of love and that it's all her fault. She blames herself for everything possible. She puts herself down in front of others, hoping they may say something complimentary back to contradict her, and even when they do, she cannot accept praise.

Helen tries to cover her 'bad qualities' by finding fault with others, which is less painful and far easier. Some will ask why Helen is such a faultfinder. Is she simply arrogant, proud and judgemental? It is far more likely to be her insecurity acting. Helen can rationalize this by saying that she finds it very painful to admit faults and failures – so she lies and makes excuses and begins to cloud what is right or wrong.

Helen has yet to meet someone who will love her as she is. Maybe she has met such a person, but it hasn't yet been communicated. This inability to communicate becomes Helen's greatest difficulty. She cannot relate well to others. She cannot open herself up to a friend. She has no way of discovering whether there are people who would accept and love her as she is, with no strings attached. And so another defence can develop – that of shyness, particularly a fear of people. She can become so bottled up in herself, that she avoids people, even though alone, she feels attacked and criticized. As a result of all this, Helen feels sorry for herself. She thinks self-pity will help her feel better but, needless to say, Helen is still miserable.

The root of Helen's problems is a lack of self-love. Erich Fromm, in his book *The Art of Loving*, gives us some idea why Helen feels the way she does:

> To be loved because of one's merit, because one deserves it, always leaves doubt; maybe I did not please the person whom I want to love me, maybe this, or that – there is always a fear that love could disappear. Furthermore, 'deserved' love easily leaves a bitter feeling that one is not loved for oneself, that one is loved only because one pleases, that one is, in the last analysis, not loved at all, but used.

The first step to healing for Helen is to know the unconditional love of God. She needs to know that God loves her, not for what she does, or the qualities that she has, or even for what she can do for him in the future. God gives each individual more dignity and worth than any other person will ever be able to give us. If you doubt that, consider the cross of Jesus Christ; there, a higher price tag is put on our life than we will ever find in our own lives. God is committed to us; he made us; he loves us; he wants us to know that. If you find it hard to love yourself, begin with the love that God has for you – *you* were worth so much that his Son Jesus Christ demonstrated his love for you when he died on the cross.

When Helen feels assured by the love God has for her, she can open up to him, for he won't reject her. So the second step to healing is for Helen to know she can be honest with God, who understands completely. The film *Ordinary People* depicts a family struggling to cope with the elder son's accidental death and the younger son's later suicide attempt. Conrad feels guilty because he lived through the accident that killed his brother. His mother, unable to express her feelings, responds with an icy silence to her surviving son, seeming to blame him for his brother's death. Her inability to show Conrad warmth and affection simply increase his self-hatred, which leads him to attempt suicide.

At some point or another, we have all struggled with areas in our past that have hurt and left us feeling battered and bruised. Through times or situations where we feel inadequate, out of our depth and not very lovable at all, we question our own self-worth. However, as we come to Jesus and share our hurt, feelings and fears, and his understanding, trust, presence and peace touch us, we can begin to be healed. It's like a wilting flower taken out of a dark, stuffy room, placed in fresh air and sunshine and given water.

The Old Testament prophet Isaiah talked about Jesus in this way:

> A bruised reed he will not break, and a smouldering wick he will not snuff out.
>
> Isaiah 42:3

We often try to figure things out alone, but we find ourselves in a fog of emotions. Many times we are too close to ourselves to see ourselves. Looking to Jesus who accepts us as we are, we can begin to be ourselves. This is when we make a leap forward towards loving ourselves, and can become an understanding person to others.

Loving ourselves means that we are in a far better position to be able to fulfil God's commandments. Jesus told us that we should 'love our neighbour as ourselves'. As we begin to love *ourselves*, can we practise love, joy, peace, patience, kindness, goodness, gentleness and forgiveness towards others. A commandment which read, 'Do not kill yourself' would seem entirely sensible, but what about destroying yourself with self-hatred? Or not forgiving yourself?

When dealing with ourselves, we sometimes feel exempt from God's law of love. Some people believe that to have a low self-esteem is appropriate. They think that being humble means feeling worthless and inadequate. Of course, none of us meets God's standards, for all of us fall short, but humility is truth and the truth is that we are loved and lovable because God, by loving us first, made us so.

> For you created my in most being;
> you knit me together in my mother's womb.
> I praise you because I am fearfully and wonderfully made.
> Psalm 139:13–14

God has created us individually. Psalm 139 describes the way in which we were wonderfully made, woven together by God. So if we feel bad about ourselves, remember that we are beautiful in his eyes. Who are we to disagree with our creator?

It is by turning and becoming children again, by opening up to God's love, by accepting and loving ourselves that we can receive grace and strength for loving God, ourselves and others.

Take It Further

Bible Study

Either Luke 15:11–32 (the Prodigal Son) *or* John 13:1–17

In John 13, note particularly verse 3. Jesus was secure in his own identity. That set him free to love us in a sacrificial way. The disciples had to let Jesus love them, before they could love others.

Talking Points

Try to think of instances in everyday life where love is not unconditional (songs, TV soaps, books and magazines where people say, 'I love you because . . . '). Discuss the love you have received from your parents or others who have had a significant role to play in your life. Was it conditional or unconditional?

What might it mean to love yourself? What's the difference between proper self-love and self-centredness? Why should you love yourself?

How does not loving yourself make it difficult for you to love others?

For Action

Write a list of what you think are your good points. Get a friend to look at it and tell you what you have missed off. Thank God for making you such a wonderful (though imperfect and sinful at times!) person.

Try to list all the ways in which God has shown 'unconditional' love for us.

Chapter 3

Guilty Chains and Broken Boundaries

Past mistakes and their consequences leave many people swamped and bound by imprisoning feelings of guilt. They cannot see beyond their failings and feel desperately unworthy. They cannot love themselves, or believe that God loves them, and so they are not able to receive the love of others. Barriers are put up; outer layers created to mask the guilty conscience. They push people away believing that if others saw them on the inside they would be shocked and reject them. At times, we can all feel so burdened by our regrets that the guilt builds up and can easily become intoxicating. Sexuality is probably the biggest source of guilt, failure and condemnation.

Some people believe that these feelings of guilt are God's way of punishing them, but they are mistaken. Feelings of guilt that lead to other negative emotions are not from God. They don't set us free as God intends us to be. The first negative emotion experienced by humankind was when Adam and Eve were ashamed by their nakedness.

Their feelings of shame, like ours, were an internal

response to what they had done. Instead of leading to repentance, Adam and Eve's guilt led to the negative action of hiding, to try and cover up and escape God's punishment. Feeling guilty is an internal emotional conflict arising out of something we have done, said or thought that we know is wrong.

There are several types of guilt. First, there is legal guilt. If, for example, we break the law of the land, we are guilty and it doesn't matter how we feel about it. A court doesn't meet to decide how guilty the person should feel. They meet to determine the guilt or innocence of the person before the law of the land. Past actions are judged against the law. Right and wrong don't have anything to do with feelings of remorse or innocence.

Secondly, there is psychological guilt. As a result of despair, people who have done nothing wrong may imagine that they have committed the unforgivable sin, or that they are so evil, the world is contaminated by their presence. People in this condition need specialized professional help and counsel.

Thirdly, there is theological guilt. With the whole of humanity, we stand guilty before God. Like legal guilt, this is objective – we are guilty regardless of our feelings. We are in the wrong before God – because of our actions, 'For all have sinned, all fall short of God's glorious standard' (Romans 3:23, NLT).

There is only one way to deal with this guilt and that is through Jesus Christ. He died on the cross to take the punishment for all our sin and guilt. He died so that we can be forgiven and therefore we do not need to carry the weight of our own sin. If we have accepted this message, no matter how much we have sinned or rebelled against God, we can be 'washed clean' and declared 'not guilty' by God. We are forgiven before God.

However, even having accepted the truth of Jesus

dying on the cross to purchase for us forgiveness, it is still hard to move on in the knowledge of our continuing weaknesses – knowing that however hard we try and whatever our resolutions might be we still have to come back again and again having made the same old mistakes. We can all identify with the Apostle Paul's frustrated experience of finding himself doing wrong things he didn't want to do.

> I don't understand myself at all, for I really want to do what is right, but I don't do it. Instead, I do the very thing I hate.
>
> Romans 7:15, NLT

The Bible doesn't only talk of the strong and the faithful 'heroes of the faith' who seemed to be able to resist all temptation put in their paths. No, God shows us the stories of those who did mess up and had to deal with failure and disappointment. Those who, like us, struggle, fail and do let God down.

The night before Jesus died, in the Garden of Gethsemane, he looked for support and comfort from his closest friends. They knew and understood this – yet they failed him.

> Then Jesus went with his disciples to a place called Gethsemane, and he said to them, 'Sit here while I go over there and pray.' . . . he began to be sorrowful and troubled. Then he said to them, 'My soul is overwhelmed with sorrow to the point of death. Stay here and keep watch with me.' Going a little farther, he fell with his face to the ground and prayed, 'My Father, if it is possible, may this cup be taken from me. Yet not as I will, but as you will.' Then he returned to his disciples and found them sleeping. 'Could you men not keep watch, with me for one hour?' he asked Peter. 'Watch and pray so that you will not fall into temptation.

The spirit is willing, but the body is weak.'

Matthew 26:36–41

It is the idea of 'willing spirits but weak flesh' that is paralleled with the young couple in love who break the boundaries. Many of us have broken promises; have failed slightly and seriously in honesty, self-control and sex. Many novels and films take as their theme the inner conflict within people. In the film *Bridget Jones's Diary*, Bridget is torn between the reserved, stiff barrister, Mark Darcy, and her flamboyant boss, Daniel Cleaver. Darcy is obviously the suitor who, in his honest and honourable advances, would care for her lovingly, but with Daniel the relationship is clearly driven by sex.

The devil endeavours to tempt us and no one, not even the godliest saint, is immune from this. For those who think they are, Paul issues this warning: 'If you think you are standing strong, be careful, for you, too, may fall into the same sin' (1 Corinthians 10:12, NLT).

In the realm of sexual activity, many people are caught off guard in a moment of weakness – Christians as well as church leaders – and get themselves into compromising situations while counselling or working with members of the opposite sex. When we hear of such stories we must never feel smug or superior or hear ourselves say, 'I would never do that,' but rather, 'There, but for the grace of God, go I.' So this chapter is relevant to all of us.

Despite 'willing spirits', Christians can easily slip into sexual sin. They never set out to fall; they fall slowly. Our failures can be divided into two groups – temporary mistakes and permanent ones. In the permanent ones we can do one of three things: we can give in, with feelings of defeat and despair, or rebel and keep on sinning or even confess our failure, but without real repentance. This is like promising our parents that we'll work hard for our exams, just to keep them off our back. It is simply a defence to allow us to keep on doing what we want and avoid real change. Basically, with permanent mistakes we just give up, fail to learn from them, lock ourselves into self-pity, refuse to forgive ourselves and reject God's forgiveness, mercy and grace.

With the temporary failures we do learn, change and move on. We forgive others and ourselves and come to Christ for forgiveness and strength for the future. Our errors may be huge, but if we rise above them, then the failure is not permanent. It was Winston Churchill who said:

> Success is never final, failure is never fatal – it's courage that counts.

It can be our decision to have the courage to come back to God, knowing that his love and forgiveness is bigger than our biggest mess-up. If we allow God to teach and refine us through our mistakes, some good can come out of them.

Let us consider a girl called Emma. She comes from a Christian family. Her parents, grandparents and siblings are all Christians. Her family and the church have drummed the Bible guidelines concerning sex into her. She finds the over-emphasis slightly irritating, but inwardly accepts the teaching of virginity until marriage. In fact she really respects it and looks down on other girls at school who have a reputation for sleeping around. 'How stupid of them – I would never do those things!' Emma thinks to herself.

It is then that Emma starts seeing Phil, casually at first, but then it develops into something more serious. Phil is really fond of Emma and tells her so often. Phil is also a Christian, but feels that the Christian boundaries are unrealistic restrictions. If sex is so wonderful, how can it be wrong? Circumstances finally combine to present a situation where Emma begins to surrender to Phil's encouragement for sex. She stops herself at heavy petting. But on the next occasion Emma gives herself entirely.

Phil leaves and she closes her bedroom door. Her eyes well up with tears. She has lost her virginity and it all happened so quickly. She doesn't even know if she loves Phil. She feels guilty, is unable to sleep that night and her conscience continues to torment her thereafter.

Was it a temporary setback or permanent setback for Emma? It all depends on her reaction. It could very easily become a slope on the way to continual sexual activity. Or it could be a stepping-stone to move on and learn from the situation, to be more humble and understanding of those 'fallen girls' at school. If she can become a warmer, more forgiving individual then Emma's lapse was serious, but only temporary.

What to do with Broken Boundaries

1. Self-forgiveness

To forgive ourselves is vital. Unless we do, we will spend the rest of our lives constantly re-living the past and getting disheartened by focusing too much on our feelings of guilt. This is not a healthy position to be in. So:

a. Let's not make excuses for failure. Trying to justify ourselves and blame other people simply evades the problem; instead, we should admit that we made a mistake.

b. Evaluate our failure and learn from it. Be objective. Was drink involved? Keeping the boundaries is hard enough without drinking. How late was it? Being tired means a weaker will. Was it because we were down or lonely? Often, at the end of a frustrating week one can want to seek physical comfort and relief. Was it after an argument? Disagreements can produce a compelling drive to express an apology to each other physically. We must learn from our errors and the things that helped cause them in order to be on guard, wise and alert in the future.

Jesus' words to the woman taken in adultery are helpful here:

> 'Teacher,' they said to Jesus, 'this woman was caught in the very act of adultery. The law of Moses says to stone her. What do you say?' . . . 'Let those who have never sinned throw the first stones!' . . . When the accusers heard this, they slipped away one by one, beginning with the oldest, until only Jesus was left in the middle of the crowd with the woman. Then Jesus stood up again and said to her, 'Where are your accusers? Didn't even one of them condemn you?' 'No, Lord,' she said. And Jesus said, 'Neither do I. Go and sin no more.'
>
> John 8:4–11, NLT

Jesus was sensitive, simple and specific. He forgave the woman but expected her to learn from her error and not to do it again.

2. Receive God's forgiveness

We have many accounts of people's failings in the Bible, including the story of David and his adultery with Bathsheba (2 Samuel 11–12). Here we have David, the king anointed by God, who sent his soldiers out into battle while he remained in Jerusalem and . . .

One evening David got up from his bed and walked around
on the roof of the palace. From the roof he saw a woman
bathing. The woman was very beautiful, and David sent
someone to find out about her. The man said, 'Isn't this
Bathsheba, the daughter of Eliam and the wife of Uriah the
Hittite?' Then David sent messengers to get her. She came to
him, and he slept with her. . . . Then she went back home.
The woman conceived and sent word to David, saying, 'I am
pregnant.'

2 Samuel 11:2–5

So David then summoned Uriah, her husband, from the
battlefront. He hoped he would sleep with his wife and
remove any suspicion from the king, of being the child's
father. But Uriah was so noble a soldier he felt that he
could not go home and eat, drink and sleep with his wife
while his friends were in the middle of a battle. David
then invited Uriah to his palace, gave him food and drink
and 'made him drunk' and yet Uriah still didn't go to his
wife.

The king then sent Uriah back to the battle with a letter
for his commander. The letter instructed the commander
to place Uriah in the front line, where the fighting was
hardest and most dangerous, so that he would be 'struck
down and die'. This happened.

When Uriah's wife heard that her husband was dead, she
mourned for him. After the time of mourning was over,
David had her brought to his house, and she became his
wife and bore him a son. But the thing David had done
displeased the Lord.

2 Samuel 11:26–27

God sent the prophet Nathan to the king. Nathan told
David a story about two men, one rich the other poor.

The rich man took from the poor one the only thing he owned, a small lamb.

> David burned with anger against the rich man and said to Nathan, 'As surely as the Lord lives, the man who did this deserves to die! He must pay for that lamb four times over, because he did such a thing.'
>
> 2 Samuel 12:5–6

David did not see the parallel between this story and his own sin. So Nathan drove the point home and said to the king:

> 'You are the man! This is what the Lord, the God of Israel says: ' I anointed you king over Israel: and I delivered you from the hand of Saul. . . . Why did you despise the word of the Lord by doing what is evil in his eyes?'
>
> 2 Samuel 12:7,9

Nathan continued and eventually David said, 'I have sinned against the Lord.' Nathan then spoke of God's forgiveness, but added that a continuing punishment would afflict David because of his sin.

> 'The Lord has taken away your sin. You are not going to die. But because by doing this you have made the enemies of the Lord show utter contempt, the son born to you will die.'
>
> 2 Samuel 12:13–14

And so today we wander away from God, eventually turning back to him for forgiveness and mercy, but often there is a residue – not necessarily, as with David, the death of a child, but anguish of conscience.

We can find comfort in the New Testament. We have seventeen different instances in which Jesus forgave a

sinner and gave mercy and grace. In Luke's Gospel, his
critics said: 'This man welcomes sinners, and eats with
them.' Jesus said, 'I tell you . . . there is more rejoicing in
heaven over one sinner who repents than over ninety-
nine righteous persons who do not need to report.' (Luke
15:2,7).

We also have a hope. In 1 Corinthians, Paul talks to the
church in Corinth which was renowned in the ancient
world for corruption and sexual promiscuity. The church
contained ex-adulterers, ex-prostitutes, thieves, drunk-
ards and many more. The Corinthians, however, knew
that their former lifestyle was in the past and they had
been able to change because:

> There was a time when some of you were just like that, but
> now your sins have been washed away, and you have been
> set apart for God. You have been made right with God
> because of what the Lord Jesus Christ and the Spirit of our
> God have done for you.
>
> 1 Corinthians 6:11, NLT

This is very encouraging but, even so, for many of us,
forgiving ourselves and receiving God's forgiveness still
leaves room for our painful feelings of guilt and regret.

3. Confession

I have found that unburdening a past error to someone
else seems to relieve and release me from a burden and
brings healing and peace. It also makes it easier to forgive
myself. It is often very cathartic to confess.

There is a story in Luke's Gospel chapter 7 where a
religious leader called Simon invited Jesus to have dinner
with him. Jesus accepted the invitation and arrived at his
home. Distinguished guests were normally offered

specific courtesies, but Simon failed to offer these. The guest's feet would be washed; he would be embraced and kissed by the master of the house and his head sprinkled with perfume before he sat down at the table. Guests sat on cushions and would be served by servants in a rich household like Simon's. Banquets were also semi-public affairs in which other interested persons were free to enter, observe what was happening, admire the food and listen to conversation. One such interested person was a woman who was a prostitute.

She arrived equipped with 'an alabaster jar of perfume' and immediately 'she began to wet his feet with her tears. Then she wiped them with her tears, kissed them and poured perfume on them.' What she was doing not only puzzled the host, Simon, but upset him and he said to himself: 'If this man [Jesus] were a prophet, he would know who is touching him and what kind of woman she is – that she is a sinner.'

As soon as Simon *thought* this, Jesus said, 'That's an interesting thought you had!' Well, actually, he said:

> 'Simon, I have something to tell you. . . . Two men owed money to a certain money-lender. One owed him five hundred denarii [a denarius was a coin worth about a day's wages], and the other fifty. Neither of them had the money to pay him back, so he cancelled the debts of both. Now which of them loved him more?'

The answer was obvious. Simon replied, 'I suppose the one who had the bigger debt cancelled.' 'You have judged correctly,' Jesus said.

Then he turned towards the woman and said to Simon:

> 'Do you see this woman? I came into your house. You did not give me any water for my feet, but she wet my feet with

her tears and wiped them with her hair. You did not give me a kiss, but this woman, from the time I entered has not stopped kissing my feet. You did not put oil on my head, but she has poured perfume on my feet. Therefore, I tell you, her many sins have been forgiven – for she loved much.'

Jesus then turned to the woman and said, 'Your sins are forgiven.' The other guests began to say among themselves, 'Who is this who even forgives sins?' And Jesus continued, applying further forgiving oil upon the repentant women, 'Your faith has saved you; go in peace.'

If you are in the dilemma of 'knowing you are forgiven and yet not feeling forgiven', speak to someone about it. Go to your minister or church leader and seek advice or recommendation as to whom to see.

Why not even write a letter to God, confessing exactly what you have done and how you feel? Express all your feelings of guilt and regret on paper. Then scrunch the piece of paper up and take it outside and burn it, or rip it into little shreds. And read Psalm 103:12, NLT:

He has removed our rebellious acts
as far away from us as the east is from the west.

Another helpful passage to read is 2 Corinthians 5:16–21.

Take It Further

Bible Study

1 Corinthians 10:13; Matthew 18:15–17; Galatians 6:1–2; 1 John 1:8–9.

Talking Points

Can you remember the three types of guilt described in this chapter?

Everyone has a breaking point. Given the right conditions, each of us is capable of breaking all of the commandments. What areas do you think are vulnerable in your life? What is liable to happen if you are unaware of your vulnerability? Think of some examples.
   What promises does God make in the verses above

(a) When you are facing temptation?
(b) When you have failed?

What actions must we take to gain the benefit of these promises?

When other people fall into sin, how should we respond?

For Action

(a) Many Christian young people in the United States are taking part in the 'True Love Waits' movement, by making a solemn pledge not to have sex before marriage. Is this something you might consider?

(b) Talk about what standards you want to uphold in a relationship. With a few friends, make a decision to support one another in prayer and friendship in the future.

(c) If you have already overstepped God's mark through premarital sex, show your repentance by finding a counsellor or Christian leader of your own sex whom you can trust, confessing to them, and asking them to pray for you to be strengthened in this area of weakness.

Dating

Review the physical side of your relationship. Is there any aspect of your behaviour that either of you feels guilty or unhappy about? Ask for God's forgiveness together.

Note for Leaders

You may be the recipient of some confessions as a result of these exercises. If so, please follow carefully the guidelines in the Appendix at the back of the book.

Chapter 4

The Pains and Pleasures of Growing Up

Adolescence is an internal revolution; it is the period in life between the beginning of sexual growth and the completion of physical maturity. Very roughly, this covers the teenage years and it is one of the most exciting but demanding phases of life. It is the transition from childhood to adulthood and it involves development and emotional maturation.

The age range of adolescence is wide. It can start from as early as ten years old and eighteen usually completes it. These are the overall limits – it doesn't last for eight years!

Adolescence is a rapidly changing period of life. One moves from being a child to an adult – a move towards freedom, responsibility and independence. This period of adolescence can bring some momentous jumps forward to maturity and adulthood and there can also be some temporary retreats to being a child – like thumb-sucking or cuddling a teddy bear or a special blanket. Emotions are also unstable and small things can catapult so many different feelings; we find it hard enough to understand ourselves and know for certain that no one around us does!

Adjustment to this period of change in one's life varies from person to person and is based on an almost limitless number of factors. There exist two opposed and conflicting attitudes and emotions. On the one hand, the adolescent dreams confidently with good hopes and expectations and is pretty elated by the prospects ahead. On the other hand there is fear, timidity, lack of self-confidence and also pessimism, a tendency to expect the worst and see the worst in all things. There is an intense longing to be physically and mentally strong and mature, but the adolescent can feel that he or she is not getting anywhere at all.

Interlinked naturally into this period of adolescence is sex. New desires surface. Girls sense that boys are fascinating and desirable. The boy becomes conscious that girls are attractive and magnetic! As these urges are so new, they arouse curiosity. The teenager becomes fascinated, and some teenagers become totally fascinated and obsessed.

Tears, worry, shame and heartbreak often cloud this period of life, and progress towards direction and control of the sexual drive can be rough.

Dr Marc Oraison in his book *Learning to Love* reports that 95 per cent of males between thirteen and twenty-five years of age go through periods of frequent masturbation (stimulation of the genitals to orgasm). With girls, about 50 per cent masturbate. The periods vary in length, sometimes lasting only a few months, sometimes continuing for many years.

Masturbation

In the past, masturbation was surrounded by an unbelievable number of myths. It was said to cause acne, dark rings around the eyes, nosebleeds, asthma and insanity. Medical research today rejects all such myths.

What should our attitude be towards masturbation?

Some Christian speakers have condemned it, without any reasons being given. One speaker I heard put it like this: 'You know those secret sins, don't you? You know what I am talking about. Those dirty, dark, personal pollutions.' Others have written chapters in books titled, 'Masturbation is Sin.'

Here are my conclusions in considering my own life, a number of other people – both male and female – who my wife and I have talked with, and my understanding of the Bible.

Firstly, there is no reference to masturbation in the Bible. Two passages that have been used against masturbation are Genesis 38:8–11 and 1 Corinthians 6:9–10. These two passages have nothing to do with masturbation. The Genesis story is quite clear – Onan's sin was not masturbation. The Corinthians passage was translated in the King James Version as 'abusers of themselves'. This was a mistranslation and has been correctly translated in all modern versions of the Bible as 'homosexuals'.

It is interesting that sexual sins such as fornication, adultery, homosexuality and bestiality are listed in the Bible and condemned. So if masturbation is a sin, why is it not listed with those already mentioned? Now of course we must be careful about this kind of logic; just because it is not mentioned in the Bible is not our guarantee that it is OK.

Secondly, from a medical position, we know that there

is no mental or physical harm in masturbation, so there are no moral arguments for health reasons.

Thirdly, when masturbation is accompanied by sexual fantasies, it clearly comes under the condemnation of Christ's words about mental adultery in Matthew 5:27–28:

> You have heard that it was said, 'Do not commit adultery.' But I tell you that anyone who looks at a woman lustfully has already committed adultery with her in his heart.

Yes, I know you can masturbate without fantasy and lust, but masturbation while thinking about physics isn't easy!

Fourthly, when masturbation with or without lust becomes an emotional substitute for personal relationships with both sexes (i.e. friends) and when masturbation is used as a way of escaping from the pressures of frustration and loneliness, then it could be unhealthy and therefore inappropriate from a Christian standpoint.

There is a very big difference between masturbation as an occasional and temporary way of relieving normal sexual build-up, particularly during adolescence, and masturbation as a compulsive, enslaving habit. In this case, masturbation is really only a symptom of deeper problems – possibly deep-seated resentments, inability to cope with frustration and anxiety, a sense of inadequacy and inability to relate to people, especially those of the opposite sex.

If this is a problem in your life, I've no doubt you have tried prayer and reading the Bible, with the sole result that you feel worse than ever for making promises to God that you 'will never do it again.' Those promises have no doubt been broken over and over again. Pray positively rather than negatively. Thank the Lord for loving you and healing you and helping you with all your concerns.

This kind of praying and trust will break the vicious circle of guilt and despair you might be in.

Secondly, socialize, don't fantasize. Make friends, be bold, and get to know people of both sexes. Get involved with things at church and beyond. If you like a particular sport, join a club. Benefit from music, the arts and entertainment with friends. I have known people who had masturbated compulsively, but when they began to look outwards, masturbation was reduced to just an occasional means of relieving sexual tensions which may eventually cease altogether.

The true joys of making friends, finding companionship or having a dating relationship can replace masturbation, which is only ever a poor substitute.

Sexuality and Homosexuality

Growing up can also be a time where people can become confused about their sexuality. In our modern climate, sexual deviation and homosexuality have become not just tolerated, but seen as an equally valid alternative to heterosexual practice. Before the 1960s homosexual practice was regarded with immense suspicion and homosexuals were marginalized in 'public society'. Now, their public profile has changed dramatically; TV, film and art, pop and celebrity culture all seem to endorse the lifestyle. Universities put on gay and bi-sexual nights and thriving societies exist to support homosexual practice. In everyday city life, having a less than positive response is quickly regarded as 'homophobic' and ranks alongside sexism and racism as 'politically incorrect' and narrow-minded.

The Bible talks about homosexuality and it is listed with other acts of sexual immorality. Despite the pressures of society, we must still take seriously what the Bible says on the subject: that it is a distortion of God's created order and contrary to God's law. God's intended purposes for sex are very clear: for the deepening of an intimate relationship between husband and wife and for the creation of children. Homosexual practice is listed in the Bible as a wrong form of sex, alongside adultery, rape, prostitution and incest.

This issue is, however, the same as every other, in the sense that what we know in theory can be far harder to put into practice. In the case of homosexuality, there are some who are trapped in an intense personal struggle. Alongside the more positive view of gay relationships has come the idea that being 'gay' is somehow inherent in one's nature, inescapable and unavoidable. Those who are actively gay might insist that they have no choice, it is simply the way they are and there is no point trying to suppress these feelings; you either submit to your 'true' nature or spend your life struggling against it in denial.

This may not be altogether wrong. It might not necessarily feel like a choice they have actively made, but in reality their actions are the result of a variety of influences; there are some biological and genetic characteristics which might contribute to a male feeling 'different'. These might be an awareness of beauty in males as well as females or a more sensitive and creative nature. Childhood experiences can also have resulted in men feeling alienated from other men (possibly the absence of a strong father figure or a past of sexual abuse). These influences may push people into a direction that they feel is inevitable (and in their minds, no longer a choice).

It is not, however, an inescapable destiny any more than frequent drug-use or alcoholism might seem like the only option to the depressed. After all, in reality, the temptation of a homosexual isn't that different from the temptation of a strongly sexed heterosexual man who lusts after a woman who is not his wife and might be tempted towards an adulterous relationship with her.

If this is a struggle for you, then do seek help to be able to address the underlying problems – find a Christian counsellor or church leader you can trust and talk with. The personal and internal conflict can seem so real and excruciatingly difficult, and it is impossible to deal with alone.

For Christians, we must be sensitive, but strong. The rising influx of gay culture has influenced some 'Christian' opinion and there is much debate, particularly among some church leaders, over its legitimacy. We should honour biblical principles and regard homo-sexuality as contrary to God's purposes, yet be careful not to marginalize or judge. We are called first to love and accept those around us and *only* then to engage with issues where opinion is divided. As we have seen previously, God has given us his grace and forgiveness to heal the hurts in our past which are preventing us from living his way. Let me remind you of the Dietrich Bonhoeffer quote from the preface: 'Remember, it is possible to have a fulfilled life even if there are many unfulfilled desires.'

Take It Further

Bible Study

2 Samuel 11 (David and Bathsheba); Matthew 5:27–30.

Talking Points

Discuss the problems of being an adolescent. What does it feel like? If you are older, exercise your memory to reminisce about some of your adolescent problems and heartaches.

For adolescents
Where and how do the greatest sexual temptations occur? What can you do to avoid them?

For non-adolescents
Do you think young people today have it easier or more difficult? How can we help the young people we know?

Why is lust wrong? Is it always sexual, or can it take other forms?

How can you help people of the opposite sex not to have difficulties with lust when you are around? How can you keep a pure attitude to people of the opposite sex yourself? What is the difference between admiration, appreciation and lust?

For Action

Practise looking at other people as God's creations, thanking him for the things you appreciate about them, without wanting to use them to meet your own needs.

Discern where you have adopted a worldly standard and work out ways you can reverse it.

Pray for any people you know who are going through adolescence at the moment, and for those you know who are working with them as youth workers or teachers.

Chapter 5

Going Out

The idea of 'dating' has changed much over the years. In the past there was significant family interaction and parental involvement. Most courtships took place in the home; prospective 'suitors' would come to visit and, no doubt, have been closely observed by critical eyes! The rise of transport, especially cars, means that dating has moved away from the home and there is far less parental involvement. Some cars have even become bedrooms on wheels, with obvious impact on dating!

In addition, young people have become more independent and reduced parental involvement even more. After World War Two, voices began to speak of right and wrong in the area of marriage and the family. Many began to believe and follow the teachings of Sigmund Freud, Margaret Mead and Alfred Kinsey. These voices endeavoured to replace God and the Bible as the authority in relationships between the sexes and in human conduct.

So instead of looking towards what the Bible teaches on the matter, there were studies, surveys and philosophies that taught what the practices of normal individuals 'should be'. Marriage was considered unfashionable and so 'trial marriages' became acceptable alternatives. Dating designed to lead to life-long marriage was obviously irrelevant if marriage itself was obsolete.

It is a myth that cohabitation is the best preparation for marriage. Co-habitation requires no commitment to permanency – the hardest requirement of marriage. The reality is that the average duration of cohabitation among single women in 2002[1] was nineteen months (and they were often left as lone parents). Couples who have cohabited before marriage are 60 per cent more likely to be divorced than couples that did not cohabit.

During the 1960s going out was redefined again by the free love movement. Building on earlier ideas that likened marriage to slavery, it moved on to describe women as victims. Traditional female and male roles needed redefining. Women would no longer accept the leadership of men. Women deserved equality and liberation.

All this has affected attitudes to dating and marriage. Marriages don't just happen. They have to be prepared for and planned for like other major life decisions, but ironically many do not see the value of this and millions change partners as quickly as others change jobs.

In the first book of the Bible we read:

> God created man in his own image, in the image of God he created him; male and female he created them.
>
> Genesis 1:27

This statement is the linchpin and cornerstone of understanding male-female relationships. Notice that all

---

[1] Office of Population Census and Surveys.

humankind, both male and female, were created in God's image. God made the male and the female to complement each other perfectly. This is obvious in the sexual union. Reading further in the Genesis account:

> For this reason a man will leave his father and mother and be united to his wife, and they will become one flesh.
>
> Genesis 2:24

This is a picture of the complete and total union of the two, male and female, in mind, body, emotion and spirit.

When a man and a woman commit themselves to each other in marriage, they commit themselves to sharing all of life's experiences. The original word used for united, literally means 'stick to' and 'be welded to'. Clearly God intended that a man and a woman should leave their parents and marry. Their new relationship is to supersede even the attachment to their blood relatives.

It is good to take an honest look at our present ideas and beliefs regarding love and marriage. We are a product of what we have been taught by the society around us. But, our beliefs and moral values may be in conflict with the teaching of God's word, the Bible.

However, it is not always that simple. There is no talk of dating in the Bible – people didn't 'go out' to the cinema. Most of the marriages were arranged and some men had several wives.

What should our ideas be about going out?

So . . . there is somebody you really like, but should you go out with them? A few suggestions to ponder on:

1. Think about it

The pressure to be a couple is huge. But don't be pressured into it. Someone showing an interest in you, although it might be flattering, is not enough to warrant going out with them. Have a think. Do you really like this person, or is it the idea of being in a relationship that appeals to you the most? Is it just a status symbol – an accessory? A young friend of mine who went to a comprehensive school told me that the most important status symbol was to have a girlfriend from the girls' private school on the other side of town. It didn't matter whether there was an attraction – you just went out with them.

Another myth is that having many sexual partners means you are a success. In reality, young people who are emotionally secure and confident don't need to bolster their feelings of popularity with superficial fulfilment, as the emotional pain involved damages their self-respect. Research among teenagers[2] showed that the main reason for teenagers having sex was perceived by them to be peer pressure.

Think about the person's personality. What qualities are you attracted to in them? What are their interests? What have you in common? Think about more than physical attraction – wanting to kiss someone is not a reason to go out with them. And don't just go out with them *because* you've kissed them. I don't believe that you need to know if you're going to marry someone before you go out with them. However, if there are obvious reasons why you *could not* marry them, then you should think again. A relationship without a future is pointless and simply a means by which you and your partner will inevitably get hurt.

Be wary at those parties where friends 'pair off' and disappear into a dark room. Although it can be tempting

---

[2] 'American Teens Speak: Sex, Myth, TV and Birth Control' (*The Planned Parenthood Poll* Louis and Associates).

to enjoy an easy thrill with 'no strings attached' for just one night, resist it. Think about it before you do.

There's no need to rush into it. Give it some serious thought.

2. *Pray about it*

Commit your desires, dreams and aspirations to God. Ask him what he thinks. He cares for you and knows what's best for you. Let him guide you.

3. *Talk to a friend*

It's always good to talk about what's on our mind. If you have a good, trustworthy friend, ask them what they think. Our friends know us very well – they can often be good sounding boards and listeners – it is also a way to order our thoughts in our own head. If you don't feel you can talk to a friend your own age, talk to an adult.

If you still think you'd like to go out with them . . .

4. *Talk to them about it!*

First Love

The novel *Seventeenth Summer* by Maureen Daly is the story of Angie Morrow's first love for a boy called Jack. It began and ended during their seventeenth summer. Angie describes what happened to her during that summer when she was seventeen:

> I don't know why I'm telling you all this. Maybe you'll think I'm being silly. But I'm not, really, because this is important. You see, it was different! It wasn't just because it was Jack

and me either – it was something more than that. It wasn't
the way it's written in magazine stories where the boy's
family always tease him about liking a girl and he gets
embarrassed and stutters. And it wasn't silly, like sometimes
when girls sit in school and write a boy's name all over the
margins of their papers. I never even wrote Jack's name at all
till I sent him a postcard that weekend I went away. And it
wasn't puppy love or infatuation or love at first sight or
anything that people always talk about and laugh. Maybe
you don't know just what I mean. I can't really explain it –
it's so hard to put into words but – well, it was just
something I'd never felt before. Something I'd never ever
known. People can't tell you about things like that; you have
to find them out for yourself. That's why it is so important.

Falling in love can be one of the most overwhelming,
electrifying, breathtaking, hair-raising, blood-tingling
events in a person's life. It is so exciting, but – we still need
to go beyond surface feelings. A first love can so easily be
blind because it is so heavily bound up with emotion.
Strong feelings for the other can cause us to lose sight of
reality and therefore so easily see qualities in the partner
that in fact do not exist. They are normally a projection of
what we want to see. The 'crush' or the 'glow' does not
always last and when unpleasant qualities of the partner
appear, it becomes obviously apparent that marriage
demands a deeper, stronger love (*agape*, *storge*, *philia*) than
this emotional, physical attraction (*eros*).

It is sad that some people in this phase of first love get
engaged (and it is announced publicly) and despite
parental opposition plans to marry go ahead. Many go
into marriage with real doubts, but because of all that's
been done they feel trapped and consequently plod on.
Let me give a warning to all of you in this situation, not to
announce marriage hastily. Don't get trapped, but if you

feel you are and you have serious doubts and uncertainties, a broken engagement is better than a possible broken marriage.

The first love can, of course, be very healthy and beneficial. It enables us to be giving rather than selfish. The eighteen-year-old who tells his parents that he is in love with a girl from college may be very self-giving during this time. He may give flowers, chocolates, attention and talk for hours with her. No price is too great to pay for her. Rain, snow, miles, mean nothing.

So while you go out, a few suggestions:

1. Don't get too intense

There's no need to declare undying love on your first date. In fact I'd strongly advise you to be careful about using the word at all. Take it gently and slowly. Don't become emotionally involved too quickly. Because of loneliness and frustration, it is easy to find false comfort and security in a premature romance. It may be tempting to talk about the 'relationship' the whole time – try not to become obsessed by it. Concentrate on building a friendship so that if a romance blossoms, in time it will be built on a foundation of friendship, respect and love, not on infatuation.

2. Make time for friends

A good piece of advice I once heard is that when you start going out with someone, your circle of friends should get bigger, not smaller. Try not to spend all your time together alone, becoming reliant and totally centred on the other person. Of course, you want to spend as much time as possible with your partner, but your relationship will grow in a much more healthy way if you make time for others. And when you are with your other friends be sensitive – don't bore them with endless details about your relationship!

3. Socialize in a group

This takes the pressure off and stops the relationship from becoming too intense. Conversation is easier with more people to participate and single friends appreciate being included.

4. Talk with each other

Friendship develops through communication – talking to each other, sharing thoughts, ideas and opinions. Without this, misunderstandings can easily occur. Communication is vital.

5. Pray with each other

Take time to pray together regularly, not just about your relationship, but other things as well, and not just personal concerns. Branch out into local, national and international issues. Keeping God at the centre of your relationship will strengthen you both, drawing you closer to each other and God. Maintaining him as your focus will create the best foundation for your time together.

6. Have fun

Make the most of each other and enjoy sharing experiences. Go walking, to the cinema, museums. . . . The possibilities are endless. Seeing each other in different settings will help you to see and get to know the 'real' person.

Let's assume your best friend is of the opposite sex and

you're not going out. Just think of all the things you can do as friends. What makes you best friends? Well, bring all that into a 'going out' relationship. Through friendship, communication, having fun with each other and with other friends you will find real joy, and if romance develops for *both* of you then the physical side of the relationship can develop slowly and on the right foundation. More of that in Chapter 7!

What About Going Out With Someone Who is Not a Christian?

Any chapter on 'going out' would be incomplete if it didn't address the question that many people frequently ask. From my experience, the only reason people continually ask this question is that they want a different answer to the one they've previously heard, and thereby obtain a licence to go out with someone who doesn't hold their Christian beliefs and convictions. Anyone looking for such a sanction here will be disappointed.

Let me say at the outset that I know this is difficult, especially when Christian men, in particular, seem to be so scarce and then usually taken. But it really is worth waiting for a Christian. The problems of going out with an unbeliever are many. Often, but not always, there is conflict over the sexual side of the relationship and other behaviour where there may be a clash of priority. The biggest problem for the Christian, however, is that you wouldn't be sharing the most important person in your life, and that is Jesus. Spiritually you are on a different wavelength.

I have heard so many Christians insist that going out with someone who is not a Christian, won't change them. But the reality is that many slowly become spiritually lukewarm. Church meetings become an inconvenience and, eventually, so does church on Sundays. Spending time with their partner seems far more important. Of course, there are stories of those Christians who went out with non-Christians and they became Christians. But for every 'success' there are many who lost their faith. And you can't go out with someone just to change them.

Sometimes people rationalize their situation by saying: 'But he (or she) *does* believe in God. . . .' As the Bible says, 'Even the demons believe that. . . .' You need to choose as your life partner not just someone who believes that God exists, but a disciple of Jesus who will join you in putting God and his kingdom first – someone who will share and encourage your faith, not just let you get on with it. It can be unkind to allow a friendship with an unbeliever to go too far, even if you don't intend to marry them. You may be sure of where you stand, but if you engage their emotions only to turn them down, they may end up hurt, and may blame God for some of that hurt. It is better to make a clear stand right from the start.

If you believe that they are 'almost' a Christian and certainly very sympathetic towards your faith, then encourage them, talk to them about it and pray for them, but wait until they *are* a Christian before going out or continuing a relationship with them. This way, it is far more likely that their faith will really be their own: stronger and built on better foundations. They will have come to Christ because they believe the Christian message for themselves instead of simply to please you or in order to spend more time with you.

My advice to you is wait and trust in God for the right person at the right time – and maybe that person still needs to become a Christian.

Take It Further

Bible Study

Genesis 1:27; Genesis 3:18–24.

Look up in the following places where Genesis 3:24 is quoted in the New Testament:

Matthew 19:3–6
Mark 10:6–9
Ephesians 5:22–32

Talking Points

What is the purpose of marriage in God's plan?

This chapter comes out strongly against Christians dating non-Christians. Do you agree or disagree with the reasons given?

Do you think it is possible to have a genuinely 'platonic' friendship with a person of the opposite sex? What should you be careful about in this kind of friendship?

How do you deal with falling for 'the wrong person' (e.g. someone who is not a Christian)?

For Action

Somewhere, there *may* be a person God has for you as your lifelong partner. If not, there is a special calling he wants you to fulfil which requires you to be single. Pray that when the time comes you will know. In the meantime God will be preparing you for that time. You don't need to worry about it. When the time comes, *you will know*.

Chapter 6

Dead-End Relationships

'Breaking up' constitutes a large proportion of pastoral problems among young people in churches and many of the agony aunt column inches in magazines. They are not all the casual 'this month's girl going out of fashion' or 'last week's boyfriend backing off'. Many involve the break-up of long-term committed relationships which had entertained hopes of a future partnership.

The media love them. They make good dramas and sell newspapers. However, if you are involved, the reality is traumatic. It can be very painful.

Even if most of the pitfalls in Chapter 5 – peer pressure, status seeking, and selfishness – have been avoided and the relationship is built on a firm foundation, sometimes it can hit a dead end. Why?

James and Jess met at school and had been going out for over four years when a crunch point came for them. Everyone else presumed they were a couple for life, and they themselves felt inevitability about it. But James began to question the future seriously. He felt he'd drifted along to this point and now he was not sure that they would be compatible as a married couple. Their expectations of careers, family and roots did not seem to match. They were still devoted to each other but was that sufficient to overcome the differences that were being aired? Painful though it was after such a long relationship, he closed the door and announced a 'dead end'.

Rob and Jane had had a similar experience. Rob changed his mind daily as to whether he should propose to Jane. As advised by friends, he too had declared a 'dead end'.

These two cases were unusual in that they both had happy endings. After several months apart, each became convinced that some of their expectations of marriage had been unrealistic and they knew they did not wish to spend the rest of their lives apart from their loved one. Both couples are now happily married and working out their lives together in harmony.

Questions that clarify commitment are provided by the marriage service: 'for richer, for poorer, in sickness and in health'. Considering issues like where we are prepared to live, how we cope with the ups and downs of life, and whether we truly value the company of another person, can help test how unconditional our love for that person really is. Would I go to the ends of the earth for this person if necessary? It's not just a romantic question to test how 'gooey' you are for the other person. It's one that, when the time is right, requires a hand-on-heart answer.

Rose enjoyed Peter's company a great deal and loved spending time with him. However, she felt uncomfortable with his more serious attitude towards her. He wanted to build a relationship for life. She just wanted a good companion with no strings attached. She also found it hard to accept that he did not pursue all his talents to the full but chose to spend time with people. She felt this was ungodly. He felt it was balanced and just as important in God's eyes. She declared a 'dead end' – they were clearly not operating the relationship on the same basis and each had become a disappointment to the other.

Tom felt his feelings for Fiona had changed – he knew he didn't really love her. It wasn't fair to continue.

Although God knows why dead ends happen, it is often far from clear for those involved. He may be redirecting their energies for purposes as yet unseen.

When we sense we are at a dead end, whatever the reason, the natural reaction is to panic. Try not to. Instead, pray. Action is going to be needed, but the way in which Christians go about it needs to be honest, loving and godly.

Ephesians 4:25 tells us to 'put off falsehood and speak truthfully with one another'. But honesty begins with a look at ourselves. In many cases our dis-ease can be caused by our own upbringing, attitude and expectations.

Here are a few areas that can lead to one person's dis-ease.

Some people have an ideal in their head of the person they want to be with. They may be looking for a carbon copy of their own parent (although some people seek out a partner who is totally the opposite!) or a model of their parent's own experience. Others have a type of temperament in mind, which they feel would best compliment their own personality. When the other person doesn't fulfil their ideal, they stick to the ideal rather than the reality. Some are taught that their twenties should be used 'in God's service', unencumbered by romantic attachments. Others have been taught that an early marriage guards against 'worldly temptations' in terms of sex and career idols. God in his sovereignty likes to shake us out of both of these. His timing is the only perfect one.

A man explained to me after breaking off his engagement that he had been taught that girls were a distraction for most of the time until one found a future spouse. Having become close friends with a girl, he concluded she must therefore be the latter. Any concept of helpful friendships with the opposite sex did not feature in his mind-set.

Thank God that he knows all the things that have moulded our thinking. He can guide us through the maze, *if* our priority is to do his will.

We don't need simplistic attitudes – they can do more harm than good. I once heard an enthusiastic youth leader announce that 'going out' was not a biblical principle, to which I replied, 'neither is watching television!' Her statement made no sense because she was flagging up a policy as if it were a principle. The Bible does have clear parameters and guidelines for us to follow, but our commitment to biblical principles may be expressed in a variety of ways. Just think about it – there are Christians in all of the political parties!

There are subcultures within our churches that have their preferred policies for the right way to conduct a courtship and the best age for marriage. Sometimes these are very helpful, as long as those who promote them do not make people feel spiritually manipulated over issues where there is no clear spiritual mandate.

It is important that we study the Bible because it is a wise manual for relationships. Our conscience before God must be clear. But do not worry if your style is different from other Christian friends – what seems right for one person need not be right for another. It's whether God is pleased that matters.

Our next point of honesty is with the person concerned. With time, a healthy relationship will grow in depth and warmth. If either partner senses a dis-ease but continues to pretend the relationship is healthy, dishonesty has crept in. Once the 'dead end' sign has been spotted, we need to face up to it and act decisively.

We all dislike change, especially when it brings sadness and pain. We all hate unpleasantness and we do not like to be the cause of someone else's hurt or anger – so we delay. We tell ourselves the doubts will go away. We hope the other person will feel the tension and take the initiative. We don't want to hurt or be hurt.

We need to think long term. What would be gained from delaying? Usually nothing. Occasionally a major exam or bereavement may cause us to consider whether the other person can cope with another disappointment – such events can be genuinely loving reasons to delay. It is important to keep our intentions to ourselves until we are ready to act, as the spreading of second-hand information can be very destructive.

Thank God he knows our weaknesses – so pray for the courage to act wisely and quickly.

The cruellest, most dishonest method, which is unfortunately very prevalent among Christian men, is to say nothing. They gradually let the relationship drift by default, leaving the girl more confused than ever. This is wrong, primarily because God never treats people like that. He speaks and he speaks clearly – so should we.

So what can you do if you have felt that a dead end is approaching? You have prayed about it to make sure you were right; you have decided before God to act lovingly. Now what? Do you write or do you speak?

I think there can be no hard and fast rule here, but I do think that face-to-face contact at some point will be necessary, so that real concerns can be heard and understood. If we are to 'esteem others better than ourselves' (Philippians 2:3) we will want to give them the opportunity to ask questions, express fears and clear away misunderstandings so that they can come to terms with the situation.

Of course there is a danger that they will try to make us change our mind. Realize this and pray for loving firmness. It's not going to be easy, so stand firm from the start.

One way in which break-ups are made so much harder is through one small practical oversight – the failure to tie up loose ends.

One young couple I knew broke up with theatre tickets still in their pockets for weeks ahead and bookings for the same accommodation at a conference. The 'dropped' party not being allowed to make contact caused unnecessary extra tension and the initiator was completely unaware of the difficulties this created. A face-to-face meeting where future difficulties can be anticipated and prepared for can save a lot of extra heartache.

It is best if the initiator can make a list of practical details beforehand so these don't get overlooked in the emotional upheaval of the moment. Honesty can take many forms, but the biblical principle of love can guide us here.

What reasons will you give for ending the relationship? Read and reflect on 1 Corinthians 13:4–7 before proceeding:

> Love is patient, love is kind. It does not envy, it does not boast, it is not proud. It is not rude, it is not self-seeking, it is not easily angered, it keeps no record of wrongs. Love does not delight in evil but rejoices with truth. It always protects, always trusts, always hopes, always perseveres.

God's will should be our overriding concern and in some cases this may be the only thing you are sure of. At this point you are both extremely vulnerable. Guard your tongue – what you say and how you say it. Don't hide behind jargon like, 'God has told me . . . .' Unless you are utterly convinced that he has. This would be a breaking of the Third Commandment, taking God's name in vain.

One friend, who closed a relationship down for rather intangible reasons, then tried to rationalize it with a detailed undermining of her friend's character to 'prove' to him why the relationship would not work. This only served to rub salt into the wound. It was unnecessary and unloving.

If reasons are given – and it is helpful to have them – try to keep them objective, godly and devoid of spite. We are all sinners. None of us are perfect. Attack is not the best form of defence.

Jesus tells us to let our 'Yes be Yes' and our 'No be No' (Matthew 5:37). He is talking about genuine honesty not needing oaths. But how often is our honesty undermined by conflicting messages? Words are not the only thing that communicate. Actions shout even louder. We need to watch that our behaviour doesn't contradict what we have said (no longing embraces, last kisses, etc).

How often have you come across someone who is not 'going out' any longer but still 'hangs around' their 'Ex'? What is the 'Ex' supposed to conclude?

It may be that you have genuine second thoughts at a later date. If this is the case, you yourself need to sort this out with God. Do not involve your 'Ex' in your seesaw rides. God can cope. For them it is much harder.

One of the most loving things you can do is give the other person space in which to recover and rebuild. When Elijah suffered exhaustion and depression after his encounter with the prophets of Baal, God gave him space, sleep and food (and more sleep and food!) (1 Kings 19). When he was ready, God then set him on his feet and recommissioned him – but only after allowing him time and space to recover.

Some meetings will be unavoidable after a break-up, but if the one who makes the break can also make the space, it will be much appreciated.

On two occasions I have counselled couples to attend separate churches for a while. This may sound drastic, but it is sometimes necessary. The one who makes the break is in the stronger position. So often the passive partners are left to take themselves off to find space, unsupported by any of their old friends. They feel guilty at not being able to cope and this adds to their hurt even more.

God is personal and he created people who are personalities. Christians further believe that God is a trinity of Father, Son and Holy Spirit who live in perfect unity. As God himself enjoys a perfect relationship, he made us to live in relationships too. The only thing in his creation that God saw that was not good was when Adam was on his own. In order to be fully human, to be the pinnacle of God's creation, he had to have someone to relate to. Eve was not identical; she was complementary but she was fully equal and brought the missing factor to the creation relationship.

The greatest suffering Jesus underwent for us was that moment on the cross when he cried, 'My God, my God, why have you forsaken me?' (Mark 15:34). The Trinity was not meant to be torn apart. We who are made in God's image will hurt when we feel the pain of separation.

We don't have to feel pressurized that we 'ought to be able to cope'. Let's give each other space and allow God to move in and heal. Don't try to be a hero – give yourself space and time.

Dead ends are dead ends, but we travel on. If you drive into a cul-de-sac by mistake you don't unpack and set up camp – you turn around and look at the map.

God never leaves us in a dead end. The question for the Christian is what to do next. God points the way to the healing that he offers, the lessons we can learn and the new level of trust we can develop (Hebrews 12:5–6).

A man asked his minister to pray that he would learn patience. The minister bowed his head and prayed for a time of trouble. The astonished man interrupted him and reiterated that it was patience he needed. Unperturbed, the minister prayed again for tribulation. 'How,' he said, 'do you think God can teach you patience if you have no context in which to learn it?'

What is it God is trying to teach you through your break-up? Is it to learn forgiveness? Is it to reveal that the relationship had become more important to you than your relationship with God? Is it to learn to trust him?

Sheldon and Davy Vanauken had the most ideal marriage that a couple could hope for, but when Davy died of leukaemia, C.S. Lewis wrote to her husband and told him that he had been dealt a 'severe mercy'.

His reason was this. Sheldon thought that his ideal relationship was an end in itself. When Davy found a relationship with God, Sheldon was jealous and resented this intrusion. During Davy's illness, Sheldon recognized for the first time the God who wanted a relationship with him too.

Lewis went on to write that married couples must live for God and for others with responsibility, especially to their own children, and not exclusively for each other.

So often we are afraid to let go of friendships in case God removes them from us. It is just this sort of attitude of 'mine' that jeopardizes our relationship with God. We must not idolize or worship our relationships. We must worship God and trust him for them.

A triangle diagram can help us visualize this. If God is at the top and we are at the two base angles, the more we move towards God on the slanting sides, the closer we draw to each other. But the direction must be focused on God. If we simply draw close along the horizontal we have made no progress with God at all. The relationship has been the focus and is in danger of becoming an idol, while God is forgotten or thought irrelevant.

Another form of idolatry is shown by constant serial relationships, where the focus is the having of the relationship, rather than the person. There are many people who are in love with the idea of 'being in love': they need to have a boyfriend or girlfriend.

Through your break-up, does God want you to refocus on him? What opportunities will your new 'freedom' bring? (1 Corinthians 7:32–33).

Maybe you feel angry? The Bible tells us not to let this burn on forever (Ephesians 4:26). Now is your opportunity to experience God's healing in this area.

Try not to nurse this hurt to yourself and feel sorry for yourself. Invite God in to heal, to restore and to redirect. Don't wallow in your sadness and pity, don't just listen to sad love songs, or read old letters again, or gaze at photographs.

If you find yourself on the other side of a broken relationship, it's hard. You can feel a failure, especially if it's not the first time it's happened. Your dream seems to be shattered, your self-esteem gone.

'On the shelf' is one of the most dehumanising phrases in our vocabulary. Reject it. We are made in God's image, he loves us and he will lead us on. Our relationship with him is the most important relationship of all.

All our imperfect relationships on earth give us pictures which help us grasp something of the true nature of God.

We have ideas from God of what it's like to have a perfect father, to be co-heirs with Jesus and to be called his friend. Our relationships on earth are incomplete reflections of the greatest relationship of all. Not only is it foolish to ignore a relationship with God but it can be devastating in a crisis.

The two most common questions people ask when life is hard are: 'Does God care?' and 'Can God do anything?' The answers are definitely 'Yes' and 'Yes'! No one cares as much or has more power to help. Jesus suffered to the point of death and separation from his Father. He knows and he cares. But he also rose again and offers his love and friendship to us today.

Take It Further

Bible Study

1 Corinthians 13:4–7; Ephesians 4:25

Talking Points

Discuss further the issues involved with some of the real-life examples quoted at the beginning of the chapter. Do you know any other people who have struggled in the same way? What about your own experiences? What can we learn from these? How is it that some relationships can reach a dead end?

What principles should guide us if we believe it is right to end a relationship?

For Action

Pray for anyone you know who is struggling with a relationship at the moment. Ask God to show you ways in which you can best help them at this difficult time.

If you are in a relationship which seems to have reached a dead end, pray for the courage to resolve this in an honest and caring way which seeks God's best for you both.

Chapter 7

Why Wait Till Marriage For Sex?

One question I am often asked is, 'If we're really in love and intend to be married in the future, why can't we make love (have sexual intercourse) now?'

There is a lot of talk about premarital sex, which suggests that everyone is doing it.

In the novel *Valley of the Dolls* by Jacqueline Susann, Anne Welles dates Allen Cooper and, despite Allen's efforts to deepen the relationship, she simply cannot fall in love with him. This frustrates Allen and at dinner one evening the following conversation takes place:

'Anne, I think you're afraid of sex.'

This time she looked at him. 'I suppose you're going to tell me that I'm unawakened . . . that you will change all that.'

'Exactly.'

She sipped her drink to avoid his eyes.

'I suppose you've been told this before,' he said.

'No, I've heard it in some bad movies.'

'Dialogue is often trite because it's easier to sneer at the truth.'

'The truth?'

'That you're afraid of life – and living.'

'Is that what you think? Just because I'm not rushing into marriage with you.' There was a hint of a smile in her eyes.

'Do you think it's natural to reach twenty and still be a virgin?'

'Virginity isn't an affliction.'

'So let me give you a few facts. Most girls of twenty aren't virgins. In fact most of them have gone to bed with guys they weren't even crazy about. The curiosity and sex drive led them to try it. I don't think you've ever even had a decent necking session with a guy. How can you know you don't like something if you haven't tried it? Don't you ever have urges or feelings about anything?'

We can add Allen's claims that it is unnatural to still be a virgin at twenty to the many similar remarks that we hear from friends and from the media. In our minds, it seems hard to sift fact from fancy, to know what is right, to decide what is best. 'Waiting until marriage' – is that a medieval concept based on flawed ideas of love and sex? An idea that has long since been out-dated?

In the film *American Pie* we see four friends make a pact to overcome the collective difficulties they have experienced in losing their virginity. At a school party, Jim, Kevin, Finch and Oz devise a scheme to 'get laid' before they finish school and go to college. The final opportunity for this is the school prom, by which time they must all have had sex with someone. But as the time draws closer and the loss of their virginity becomes imminent they start to question whether they want to lose it purely for the sake of it.

We live in a time which embraces a truly liberal attitude towards sexuality. Frequent pre-marital sex has exploded in the last thirty-five years. It is not only behaviour patterns that have changed, but our attitudes too:

- In 1965 – 65 per cent of men and 69 per cent of women believed that sex before marriage was wrong.
- In 1972 – the figure had dropped dramatically to 21 per cent of men and 24 per cent of women.
- In 2002 – only 6 per cent thought that sex should be kept for marriage.[1]

A while ago, *Arena* and *New Woman*, both award-winning magazines, published the results of an extensive survey of young thinking on sex. What do you make of these?

- 20 per cent of people lose their virginity between the ages of 13 and 15.
- The majority lose it between 16 and 18.
- After the first sexual encounter, few go for six months without having sex.
- 75 per cent of men have had more than ten sexual partners.
- 73 per cent of men claimed they could have sex 'with no emotional ties'.

And perhaps the most perceptive line in the article was this: 'No one, but no one, said sex was for marriage. You completely godless lot!'

We live in a sex-permeated atmosphere. Why? When dealing with sex, society holds onto a largely utilitarian philosophy; a course of action is determined according to what will bring humans the most happiness and pleasure. Teenagers and people in their early twenties are often unsure of themselves – searching for security and striving for maturity. In addition to these factors, people who are in love also feel an intense compulsion to express physically, and sexually, their inner longings for

---

[1] *The De-moralization of Society* Alfred Knopf , New York, p.236.

tenderness. We all know the easy, temporary solution to counteract these feelings. But is the easy answer the correct one? Will sex give us the confidence we crave and strengthen mutual love in a relationship?

Well, for many people, sex has nothing to do with love. It is simply a means of satisfying desires. Tina Turner's song, 'What's Love Got To Do With It?' from the album *Private Dancer*, rings true. For many, sex has nothing to do with love. It is no more than an evening's pastime or the ultimate way to round off a night out. The lyrics from hip-hop artist Fifty Cent's song, 'In Da Club', from the album *Get Rich or Die Tryin*, reveal the attitude of many towards the sacred and intimate act of sex: 'I'm into having sex, I ain't into making love.'

These are times when our role models are no longer morally responsible.

There is a saying that 'boys offer love to get sex and girls offer sex to get love'. If this is still the case, then who loses out when the value of sex goes down? Despite the 'sexual freedom' in our society, few would attempt to argue that this has resulted in better and stronger relationships – but only in a greater quantity of broken and dissatisfying relationships.

Guidance From God

Society's stance on sex is clear, but what does God have to say about it?

As we have already seen, it is the Christian conviction that God created man and woman. He made sex for the unity and enjoyment of two people in a monogamous, lifelong relationship. God is not against sex: he created it. His guidelines are not illogical – they simply reflect the wisdom of our creator.

Sex is for that lifelong relationship which is begun when the public commitment is made to each other at the wedding ceremony. That is his ideal: sex is with one person for life. Now anything other than that is going against God's will for his creation. It is falling short of his standard and the Bible terms that as sin. We must trust that he knows what's best for us. Sex outside of marriage is wrong because it causes hurt, damaging ourselves and other people. It gives a lower quality of life than God intended for us.

God loves us. He knows what sex is for and where it is best used. The best is sex in marriage. His instructions are clear.

The Bible addresses the problem of upholding the Christian standard in a world where it is ignored and mocked. Let's look at one example: the letters of the Apostle Paul to Christians in various cities of the Mediterranean are relevant. Several of them – 1 Corinthians, Galatians and Ephesians – contain severe warnings about fornication (pre-marital sex) and adultery (extra-marital sex).

Paul was a Jew, as was Jesus. They lived in Jewish communities and breathed in the Jewish religious and ethical atmosphere. Unmarried people were supposed to be virgins. A man who slept with a woman outside marriage could be punished severely, either in a financial way or by death, depending on the circumstances. This continued into married life, so adultery could be punished by death.

Sexual ideals in the Roman world, however, especially in Greece, were not the same. It would be safe to say that chastity was nowhere esteemed in the Hellenistic world except among the Jews. Contrasting sharply with the Jewish world, in the Greek world polygamy (the practice of being married to more than one woman at the same time) had depreciated the respect for a woman. A man was free to do as he pleased without punishment. However, this was not the case with the woman. The woman became an inferior partner at home, insignificant outside the house, and stood as a second-class citizen even in the upper sections of society. Premarital or extra-marital sex for a man, married or single, was judged a minor failing, if a fault at all. Homosexuality, incest and other sexual deviations were not uncommon and often the law ignored them. The Roman world's view of women was a bit better than the Greek's picture, but nowhere near the Jewish expectations.

Therefore, Christians living in the first century at Corinth found sexual standards low. Corinth, a commercial city, was notorious as a hotbed of every kind of vice. 'To live like a Corinthian' meant complete moral collapse. A 'Corinthian girl' and a 'prostitute' were the same. Corinth was a red-light district!

Some early followers of Christ, hearing about the freedom from the Law and emphasis on the Spirit talked about in the New Testament, misunderstood, thinking that since legalism was out, so Jewish rules could be forgotten and pagan pleasures adopted. So the Apostle Paul wrote in 1 Corinthians:

> I am not writing these things to shame you, but to warn you as my beloved children.
>
> 1 Corinthians 4:14, NLT

> I can hardly believe the report about the sexual immorality going on among you.
>
> 1 Corinthians 5:1, NLT

> Don't you know that those who do wrong will have no share in the Kingdom of God? Don't fool yourselves. Those who indulge in sexual sin . . . none of these will have a share in the Kingdom of God.
>
> 1 Corinthians 6:9–10, NLT

Pretty strong words. He says that this way of living causes serious breaches, violations and transgressions in life, so serious as to exclude those who practise them from membership of the church and, ultimately, from eternal life with God. We cannot be Christ's followers and conduct ourselves along these lines. God sets higher standards for us.

But Why Does God Set These Standards?

As Christians, we will strive to live our lives for Jesus. However, at some point, we will come across certain circumstances where we will find it hard to fathom the 'mind' of God. There is no doubt about it, but some mysteries we will only understand when we get to heaven. In some areas, trying to work out God's purposes and plans for his world seem too complex for our minds.

God's commandment that we should keep sex for marriage, however, is not one of these mysteries; we do not have to look very far to see the damage that it causes. As with everything, the way that we decide to act has its consequences. It not only hurts God, but the ways in which we, too, are hurt become blindingly obvious.

The increased sexual freedom in our country has resulted in increased sexual problems. Sexually transmitted diseases are one such example. Although pregnancy can occur only as the result of intercourse during a relatively short phase of a woman's menstrual cycle, AIDS and other sexually transmitted diseases can be transmitted 365 days a year. A research scientist reported in the American scientific journal *Rubber Chemistry and Technology* that 'Latex rubber contains inherent flaws that are at least 50 times larger than the

AIDS virus – and the effectiveness of condoms for AIDS protection is actually much worse than for contraception.'

The problem of AIDS is now widespread. Last year alone, there were 5 million new infections diagnosed and 3 million people died. The reality of AIDS is so apparent, yet still its threat has not really reformed social behaviour. Today's slogan is, 'Have Safe Sex', rather than 'Wait to Have Sex'.

Unwanted babies are also the result of this sexual freedom. There have been 6 million abortions in Britain since 1967 – 600 every working day. In 2003 there were 175,600 abortions – 78 per cent of which were funded by the taxpayer. In America there have been 44 million abortions since 1973 when abortion was legalized. How can our carelessness and pleasure justify the death of these children? It is a myth that condoms make sex safe. In the course of a year, condoms have a 13–15 per cent failure rate against pregnancy. It is nearer a 20 per cent failure rate for teenagers.[2]

Equally as damaging as the health risks are the effects that sexual relationships have on us emotionally. The confusion and hurt that was considered in Chapter 6 – 'Dead-End Relationships' – are made only more acute by the added sexual dimension.

The film *Indecent Proposal* gives the message that you can't separate body and soul for a one-night stand – once you give your body, you give away something of your soul. I believe this is true.

God designed sex to bind a husband and wife together more deeply – almost like glue, binding them so strongly that they are never intended to come apart. It makes sense, therefore, that if we are to separate ourselves from

---

[2] *Condom Use and Failure*, Lancet and Kirkman.

a sexual partner, the damage is extensive and we are, quite literally, torn apart.

Noah Gordon's novel *The Rabbi* is a story about Michael Kind, a young Jewish boy – from his early childhood to becoming a Rabbi and then the years that follow.

At school he frequently kissed the girl next door, Ellen, more for thrills than for anything deeper. He almost lost his virginity with her one summer. 'I may be in love,' he entertained the idea. Later in college he lost his virginity with Edna, a young widow. This was not love, but nor was it completely unfeeling or casual sex. However, the little relationship that existed with Edna evaporated. While training to be a Rabbi, Michael and a friend met two girls and went to the friend's home (his parents were away). Michael and his friend separated with their partners into different rooms. After 'making love' with Michael, the girl called to her friend and they switched rooms. The future Rabbi was at first excited by this strange turn of events, but the coarseness of it all, the awareness that this was simply a routine, the girls had done this many times before in many places with many men, suddenly sickened him. He quickly dressed and left. Returning home, he showered with really hot water, lots of soap and much scrubbing to take the 'dirt' off.

Later in life, Michael meets Leslie at a hospital having treatment for depression. She struggles with guilt and considers herself to be an unfit wife and mother because of a sexual experience she had as a student more then twenty years previously.

It was with this boy at university I didn't even like. His mother went to school with my aunt, and to please them we went out a couple of times so we could both write home about it. I let him make love to me in his car, only once, just to see what it was like. It was simply awful. Since then I haven't enjoyed kissing a boy and I've never been able to feel passionate.

The memories of her previous sexual relationships continued to haunt her and she could not shake them off. Every person who has sexual intercourse outside marriage will not necessarily react like Michael and Leslie – but like Michael and Leslie many do suffer from guilt feelings and subsequent emotional difficulties.

Paul's understanding of sexual relations explains so clearly why many suffer emotional crises after a broken sexual relationship:

> Don't you realize that your bodies are actually parts of Christ? Should a man take his body, which belongs to Christ, and join it to a prostitute? Never! And don't you know that if a man joins himself to a prostitute, he becomes one body with her? For the Scriptures say, 'The two are united into one.'
>
> 1 Corinthians 6:15–16, NLT

The Apostle is saying that sexual relations cannot remain a merely casual affair. A oneness is formed, so close that it produces an identity of flesh. Such a union flows over into the whole being of the persons involved and cannot be limited just to surface entanglement, soon to be forgotten.

An argument frequently put forward is that those who have experienced intimate sexual relationships before marriage will be better sex partners in marriage. The belief is that if a couple don't sleep together before marriage they may not be sexually compatible and the marriage may break up. This is a myth. The reality is that all researchers since 1923 have come to the same conclusion, that premarital chastity is associated with greater sexual satisfaction and a lower incidence of separation and divorce.[3]

It must also be said that sexual intercourse before marriage is not the same as afterwards. Dr Evelyn Duvall's book *Why Wait Till Marriage?* describes concisely elements which can make premarital sex highly unfulfilling:

> First sex experiences are often disappointing. The male becomes excited too quickly. It takes time for a girl to awaken sexually. Males tend to be body-centred and females person-centred. Thus their premarital experience can be frustrating. The male may go through with it, but without the satisfaction her response would have brought him. The girl may attempt to match his enthusiasm, but be left unsatisfied, un-awakened or uneasy. . . . Because each feels a little anxious and a little guilty, the female is likely to be frigid and the male at least partially impotent. They may be left with the feeling that they are inadequate human beings when the very thing they set out to prove was their competence. Fear of discovery keeps many from full enjoyment of their intimacy. The need for concealment of premarital sexual intercourse gives little or no security to the relationship. The young pair before marriage all too often have to snatch what they can get where they can get it. The couple are left unsatisfied even after having gone through the motions of going all the way . . . .

The husband and wife, who so seal hearts and hopes together at the altar, join their bodies together in the marriage bed. Sexual intercourse deepens their

---

[3] Bancroft, *Human Sexuality and Its Problems*, Churchill Livingston, Edinburgh.

commitment to each other – it physically expresses their total union.

Building The Strong Relationships As God Intended

Now let's look at this issue from a different perspective. In the book *Bed and Board: Plain Talk about Marriage* Robert Capon offers a young couple before marriage a few principles to guide them in their courtship:

> A couple of years back there was a cartoon that showed two clams sitting at the bottom of the ocean. One of them says to the other, 'But you wouldn't buy a new car without driving it first, would you?'
>
> My premarital couple doesn't crack a smile. Not an eye blinks. As far as they are concerned, I am only supposed to be a 'minister of religion' – like in the films, the predictable vicar who thinks life is about afternoon teas and long walks. I raise the subject of premarital sex.
>
> 'What do you think you have to practise before marriage?'
> They watch me blankly.
>
> 'Well, you don't have to practise going to bed together. And you don't have to, because you can't, so forget about practising it – you'll have plenty of time later. What you really need to practise is keeping promises. Right now you wouldn't go to bed with anyone else, but later on, it's not always that clear and then those little exercises in fidelity will be worth something in terms of chastity and trust. So if you have so far been chaste, don't let anyone talk you out of it. And if you haven't been – well, cut out the compromises.'
>
> That usually produces silence. Since there is a lot of premarital gun jumping even among professing Christians, and since it is usually justified with fairly high-fluting

reasons, I feel obliged to say it. Fancy reasons or not, I tell them not only to be chaste but to be modest – to cut out not only the intercourse, but all the little semi-moral approximations to it: the heavy petting that everybody takes for granted.

Robert Capon has not mentioned Biblical principles. Instead, the couple are told that waiting for sex is the best preparation for a faithful, fulfilling and lasting marriage. I, too, believe that sexual control before marriage strengthens love.

Robert Capon emphasizes that what a couple really needs to practise before marriage is not sexual intercourse, but *keeping promises*. The essence of marriage is this – to promise, to make a vow, to offer one's heart and body to the beloved for life. There is a commitment made here before God and family and friends, to live and give in sickness and in health, for richer or for poorer, for better or for worse. It's not just a piece of paper, because God's life is present in and vital to the husband-wife relationship – it is a sacrament.

> Give honour to marriage and remain faithful to one another in marriage. God will surely judge people who are immoral and those who commit adultery.
>
> Hebrews 13:4, NLT

The sacrament of marriage is not just a ceremony that says; 'Now you are allowed to make love, with the church's blessing.' A sacrament is an event, a happening, in which God touches our lives in a special way with the power to help us become what we are meant to be. The ceremony of marriage tells others that this couple now publicly, before their Maker and their fellow men and women, vow to share each other's lives together. Only death will cut the cord which now joins them.

Many romances never reach the altar. Many people fall in love, but staying in love and seeing that love develop and produce sustained happiness is something else.

Most of us count at least a few broken hearts in the search for a love that will stand married life. A couple may believe that they are in love. But can they be sure this love will last? It may, but there is no permanent commitment. Someone once said, 'Never give your love so slightly, until you wear a wedding ring.' Couples in love at moments of tenderness and intimacy feel their relationship will never break up. But can they be certain before they vow 'until death us do part?'

Feelings can be fickle and the engagement ring can be returned. Let's say they do have sexual intercourse but later the beautiful love sours, they break up and go their separate ways – does the same pattern repeat itself with the next partner?

A successful marriage requires a spiritual, emotional and intellectual union as well as a physical one. A physical union is the easiest to obtain and should be the last to come. The other unions take time, effort and patience to develop. The physical union built on the spiritual, emotional and intellectual union can deepen and sustain them, but an overhasty arrival of the physical into courtship can hinder the growth of those more stable and permanent unions.

Wedded life is not simply going to bed together, but living together every day for the rest of our life. Out of the twenty-four hours a day, eight of them are usually spent sleeping. How many of the remaining sixteen are given to love-making?

The time for courting and engagement should be spent deepening a couple's mutual understanding of each other. They need to know each other well – likes, dislikes, understanding one another's moods, hopes, fears and failings. They need to know each other as people. As one girl commented:

> Love him, don't make love to him. It spoils everything and I regret it so much. We got caught up in each other's bodies and forgot about our minds, our ambitions, and the wonders.

Love and respect go together. It seems impossible for a person to love someone without respecting them. And communication probably heads the list as the most important ingredient in a relationship. When sex is involved, communication can often be overlooked. Without honest talking between two people, sincere friendship cannot blossom.

What is it that we are really looking for? A loving, open, totally accepting relationship; a place where one is entirely committed to the other as a person; an atmosphere of longing to please each other; a safe confine, deeply intimate and lasting? This is what God offers to us in his decree and purposes for marriage. This is where sex will work.

What more can I say? Sex is beautiful, it's great, it's God's wedding present to you on your wedding day – open it then!

But what if this advice is all coming too late for you and you've already lost your virginity? I hold out to you that in Jesus Christ there is forgiveness and the opportunity of renewing and recreating a new start. Doesn't the resurrection of Jesus prove to us and assure us that God brings new life? It is not the end. We are never outside God's love. Nothing is irredeemable to God. Re-read Chapter 3!

Let us respect God and his standards. In this day and age one of the main areas where Christians stand out is in the whole area of sex. Don't let anyone look down on you just because you're a virgin and you hold God's views on sex. Never apologize for upholding God's standards and know that God is mightily pleased with you.

Take It Further

Bible Study

1 Corinthians 6:12–7:9

Talking Points

Discuss the different ways in which a courting couple will need to grow together, e.g. mental, spiritual, sharing values, etc.

The Christian attitude to sex is often portrayed as negative and restrictive. How can we present the positive value of abstinence in today's world?

What difference does it make to regard your body as the 'temple of the Holy Spirit'?

For Action

Review some of the songs and films that are currently popular. What attitudes to sex and marriage are conveyed in them? How do these attitudes differ from the Christian view? If you allow yourself to be influenced by them, what kind of behaviour will result?

Together with a group of Christian friends, watch the film *Indecent Proposal*, or *Unfaithful*, and discuss it critically.

Chapter 8

How Far Do You Go?

We have looked at why we should wait for sex till marriage, but another question remains unanswered. How far can a couple go?

We looked earlier about growth during adolescence. Those years and the years following are aiming for maturity. Maturity in understanding and self-control. What creates growth and maturity in one area promotes it in other areas.

Toddlers and young children run around, screaming and laughing at very inopportune times; they have tantrums and throw toys around the room. As we grow older, we can no longer act in this way. We can't just let our feelings and emotions run wild or do exactly as we please – we wouldn't get very far if we did! As we mature we have to learn how to control ourselves in order to live with others. When we were very young our parents controlled our behaviour (or tried to!). Then a time comes when we endeavour to manage ourselves. Our self-control is a vital ingredient of our personality: vital in budgeting our money, managing our time and controlling our sexual behaviour. It's also encouraging (despite what Freud and others have said) that there is no evidence that self-control damages our sex lives – quite the opposite actually!

One example to illustrate this is electricity. Electricity is a powerful natural force, but running wild as lightning can burn down a building in a great blaze and create irreparable damage. Lightning can ruin in a few minutes what has taken years to build and develop. Yet lightning is natural, uncontrolled electric power. That same energy through the wires of our homes can provide light and heat. Sex, like electricity, can run wild and get out of control or, properly channelled, it can light and heat our lives. It can destroy others, hurt loved ones, or it can bless and bring joy.

Giving an answer to the question, 'How far do you go?' is delicate and difficult. If I give some practical rules, some will call it legalism. If I fail to give specifics, then others will put the book down unsatisfied, complaining that another writer has avoided the issue. This chapter is highly controversial and any position I take will invite criticism.

The question 'How far do we go?' is not a matter of getting every bit of pleasure and experience we can without offending God. Instead we should try and consider how we can best please God in this relationship. When discerning how far to go, there are several truths, which the couple should know in preparing to make a decision.

Firstly, sex is precious, as has already been said, so tampering with sex irresponsibly is serious.

Secondly, more people have wounds inflicted by sexual activity than by almost anything else. It is desperately easy to lose control and end up feeling vulnerable, dirty, worthless, used and full of regret. The other sex is not a creation for us to satisfy our sexual desires on. Put respect above all else – respect for the other person's body and respect for your own. Remember the words of the Apostle Paul:

> Don't you know that your body is the temple of the Holy Spirit, who lives in you and was given to you by God? You do not belong to yourself, for God bought you with a high price. So you must honour God with your body.
>
> 1 Corinthians 6:19–20, NLT

Thirdly, honesty is essential. Mutual, open discussion between a man and a woman is essential. One partner may discover that a specific action is too 'hot' for them – each person needs to be honest and admit these feelings.

Couples should discuss ahead of time how far to go, and if definite boundaries are established, then during times of 'passion' the stronger partner may remind the weaker one of the boundaries. If they have agreed that they will only go this far, then objective honesty is required to avoid going beyond the agreement. It is far harder if boundaries are blurred and, therefore, the game of guessing should be eliminated. No longer does he think, 'How far will she let me go?' or 'How far does she want me to go?' No longer does she think, 'How far does he expect me to go?' or 'How far does he really want me to go?' Each partner knows, because it was decided when both were cool, calm and collected.

The Internal Barometer

When a woman/man senses she/he has started to become aroused and is getting overexcited, then it is time for her/him to pause, relax and take a step back. And/or if one partner senses that the other is aroused and overexcited, the partner under better control has a responsibility to take the initiative to cool the situation down. I think we can safely say that the girl usually tends to be under better control!

How does a person know their partner is aroused? I am sure each person usually senses and recognizes the time to stop, and honesty makes it easier to understand each other's boiling point.

Guidelines

Although I do want to avoid an extreme legalism, I offer the following guidelines:

Holding hands

Hand-holding, or putting an arm around each other, is generally no problem, although with some individuals, whose affections are very easily aroused, any physical contact can trigger a whole set of powerful sexual forces.

Kissing

A kiss signifies caring. A kiss on the side of the cheek usually means friendship. A kiss on the lips means more than just friendship. Kissing can arouse easily, although the reaction is not always automatic as it depends on the kind and intensity of the kiss and the length of time the couple are kissing.

Can you kiss on your first date? This is really a question of personal preference. For some a goodnight kiss means 'Thank you for a lovely evening.' For others, it means more than thank you, something more special, so is reserved till several dates have developed that something special.

French kissing

This is an open-mouthed kiss in which you use your tongue. For some people this sort of kiss is so stimulating it's difficult to put the brakes of self-control on. For others, French kissing doesn't lead to any loss of self-control and is very pleasurable. There are no hard-and-fast rules. If you find French kissing knocks you for six and you're in danger of losing your self-control, it's simple – don't do it; save it till marriage.

Dancing

There are of course a variety of different dances, what I am addressing here is the tight, close and very intimate type of slow dancing. This is usually an excuse for holding someone's body very close to yours. Be careful. You don't have to dance so closely to someone. Think about what you are doing.

Light petting

This term generally means to touch the body over the clothing, particularly the breasts. There is an automatic reaction when a women's breasts are caressed. The presence of erectile tissue and the enlargement of the breast during excitation means that the woman's whole body can be excited through such fondling, and this can often be as satisfying to her as sexual intercourse – all because of light petting!

As for heavy petting, which involves the touching and caressing of the genitals, often leading to orgasm, it includes everything beyond light petting and short of sexual intercourse.

I believe that sexual intercourse and those things which

closely lead up to it, should be reserved for marriage. If light petting arouses and sets in motion the intricate and powerful process leading to sexual intercourse, it follows that heavy petting does so to an even greater degree and therefore should be reserved for marriage.

For those who have already gone too far, it's not too late. Be brave. Take some steps back physically and you'll find you will take steps forward in many other ways. Here are two general rules:

1. Don't touch what you haven't got.
2. Don't undress each other.

Never feel pressured to go further than you know is right and try to remain focused on building a strong friendship; don't get into the habit of getting physical as soon as you are alone.

Talk about it. Set your standards when you're talking, not while you're in the full flight of passion. Be honest, be careful, honour God with your body and you will be mightily blessed. There's no need for Christians to deny they are sexual beings, but let's honour our God. We have been bought at a price and our bodies are his. This is one of the biggest areas where Christians set a different standard from that of the world. Remember God's not a downer – he wants only what's best for us.

Take It Further

Bible Study

Song of Songs 7:1–8:4

The Song of Songs is a love poem, expressing *eros* love.

One of the reasons it is in the Bible is to show that sex is good, in the right place.

Ephesians 5:1–20; Galatians 5:19–23.

Talking Points

What do you think about the guidelines suggested in this chapter?

What might mark out a Christian viewpoint and practice from a non-Christian one? List the differences.

For Action

Think carefully about what you have read in this chapter. Consider your boundaries, so you are ready when the time comes.

If this chapter leaves you feeling there is a world of fantastic experiences you are missing out on, then sit down and make a list of all the advantages you can think of in being 'footloose and fancy free'.

Dating

Discuss the contents of this chapter and draw the lines that you believe God wants you to keep to. Together, ask him to help you keep to them, and from this time onwards, hold each other to them. Saying 'no' often conveys more real love than saying 'yes'.

Chapter 9

Single and Waiting

'Where can I find a partner?'
'Will I ever get married?'
'Am I to live my life single and lonely?'

Images of 'singleness' can sway from the extremes. On the one hand, leading a single life can be portrayed as the 'land of the free': an enviable life without burdensome responsibility and domestic restrictions; a glamorous situation bursting with opportunities and excitement. Yet, it is also the life that people seem most keen to leave behind. Its other associations are long, dark, lonely nights and a miserable state. It seems only sensible to comment at this point that neither of these stereotypes can be consistent; we know only too well that life varies – there is good and bad to be found in all situations. However, the majority of us would agree with God's proclamation, 'It is not good for man to be alone.'

The world we live in, however, does not embrace singleness. The film *Bridget Jones's Diary* seems to encapsulate many of the fears and pressures that one can feel – the fear of being alone and being lonely and the seemingly constant pressure from friends and family to 'settle down and find a nice partner'. Party invitations often require us to 'bring a partner'. Magazines are full of self-help tips on how to secure and keep the partner of your dreams. Adverts imply that the key to success in this area is using the right perfume or aftershave, whilst Internet 'pop-ups' inform you that *your* perfect date is waiting and with a simple click of the mouse button, true love is destined to come your way. Finding the right partner to marry can seem like the ultimate achievement.

The biblical view of 'singleness', however, is very different. Remaining single is, moreover, considered to be something special – a vocation. Several key people in the Bible were called by God to be single long-term.

We can probably assume that the Apostle Paul did not marry; yet he indicated the same appreciation of marriage as any of the other leaders of his day.

> Don't we have the right to bring a Christian wife along with us as the other disciples and the Lord's brothers and Peter do?
>
> 1 Corinthians 9:5, NLT

Luke, Timothy, Titus, Silas and others apparently did not marry. Yet Peter, James, Philip and others did marry. The Apostle Paul has been accused by some of being a misogynist and misogamist – two fancy words that mean a hater of women and a hater of marriage. Paul was neither. Many have misunderstood the Apostle's statement, 'It is good to live a celibate life' (1 Corinthians 7:1, NLT), although we can be sure that remaining single was a valid and respected status to have in the ancient world.

For most of us, however, the idea that God may have called us to a single life can be more than we can bear. As with many areas, society's view can often taint our own reading of situations. Most of us are raised with the expectation of marriage and raising a family deeply engrained within us. For some (particularly girls) the idea of being single and not raising a family of their own, can seem devastating and shatters childhood dreams. Many older single adults would agree that even in a church setting where there is such an emphasis on family and children's pastoral work, it is easy to feel marginalized and alienated if you are single.

We must, however, keep a right perspective on the matter. We know that if we are trying to live as a Christian we can trust God for his perfect plan for our lives. Being single at any given time may be exactly what God intends us to be and where he knows we will best be able to live a life of value for him.

But what if you are single, you want to follow Jesus Christ faithfully, and you would also like to have a partner but have not found anyone compatible to share your life with? The best answer I can give is that *the one person you can prepare for marriage is you!* While you wait for the right person there are some things you can do. It goes without saying that you pray about it. Talk to your heavenly Father honestly. Express your feelings and desires to him. Trust him because he is trustworthy, and be prepared to accept his will for your life.

In the meantime:

- If you are single . . . enjoy it! Take the time to develop yourself. Explore your own individuality. It is a good time to consider what things you value most in life and where your priorities for the future lie. If you know yourself, it can be far easier to find a partner who you are really compatible with when the time is right. If a person has never really been able to accept himself or herself, they may find it difficult to be accepted by someone else.

- Make the best of where you are at the moment. Spending time pining for anything else is a waste. Very often, we are not aware of the positives of our situations until they are taken away from us. Fulfil your interests and abilities; getting married and having children will restrict what you can do.

- Do not feel undervalued. Know that being single does not mean that you are somehow incomplete without a partner. Every person is of enormous value with or without a partner. This does not change depending on our circumstance.

- Try never to idolize a relationship. This can sometimes be difficult; especially when it's something that we don't have ourselves, but I can assure you that a boy/girlfriend is not the ultimate solution to all of life's problems. We can be led to believe that being in a close and intimate relationship can fulfil our deepest human needs. But it can't! A boy/girlfriend will not do this. Only Jesus can fill an empty hole in a person's heart – relationships will not do this, nor were they designed to do this. Relationships, alongside many other things – money, success, image, can be falsely idolized. Being in a couple should not be an ultimate 'goal' nor should remaining single be viewed as a failing of any kind. They are simply two different situations in a life where we are called to live for Jesus.

- Practise contentment. The Bible reminds us not to envy the security that someone else might have, but learn to rely solely on him and on his promises. Be content with what you have, because God has said, 'I will never fail you. I will never forsake you' (Hebrews 13:5, NLT).

- Be active and involved, where appropriate, in things that might be happening in your church or community. Meet and integrate with people. It may be the case that we are in a situation where we feel alone and isolated from people and the chances of meeting someone special seem to us to be very limited. If this is the case for you, don't worry. God is the God of the impossible and he can intervene.

There is a story in the Bible that illustrates how God can intervene for those who have prepared themselves. It is the story of Ruth – the woman who rose from obscurity to riches.

The background to the story is that Elimelech and his wife, Naomi, and two sons, Mahlon and Kilion, in order to escape drought and famine in Bethlehem, emigrated to the neighbouring country of Moab, where the people were not believers. After a while, Elimelech died and the two sons married women of Moab. Mahlon married Ruth and Kilion married Orpah. After about ten years, both Mahlon and Kilion died leaving their widows childless.

Now there were three widows living together in Moab without material resources or support, probably in poverty. They heard that conditions had improved in Bethlehem and so Naomi, the mother-in-law, decided to return to her homeland. The two younger widows, Ruth and Orpah, had to face a decision; they could stay in Moab or go back with Naomi to her homeland. Deeply attached to their mother-in-law, who had become a second mother to them and to whom they clung as their friend and counsellor, they decided to go with Naomi, but on the way they stopped and Naomi urged them to return to their own country, marry again and settle down. She did not want them to face uncertainty in a strange land. Orpah decided to go back but Ruth decided to stay with Naomi.

Ruth replied, 'Don't urge me to leave you or to turn back from you. Where you go I will go, and where you stay I will stay. Your people will be my people and your God my God. Where you die I will die, and there I will be buried. May the Lord deal with me, be it ever so severely, if anything but death separates you and me.'

Ruth 1:16–17

Ruth's declaration of love and loyalty for Naomi marks out her feelings as being unselfish and pure.

Having arrived in Bethlehem, Naomi was reminded of how her sufferings had changed her. Friends found it hard to believe that this was the beautiful woman who had left them ten years before. At that time she was clothed so well and now she appeared in poor and sorrowful dress. Her brow was wrinkled, her back bent and she had a 'foreigner' by her side.

At first it seemed as if they were to remain desolate and uncared for, but fortunately it was harvest time and the golden corn was being gathered in. Naomi and Ruth had to live. Ruth's mother-in-law was of course quite old and not able to work. So Ruth went to work in the fields of the godly landowner Boaz.

Boaz, a wealthy, single man, checked out who she was. Upon hearing the story of her love for her mother-in-law and her willingness to leave her own people, to worship the true and living God, Boaz was much impressed. He must have wondered, 'Could this be the woman I've been waiting for?' As it turns out, she was. But the story doesn't end there. It was not simply a matter of a man and a woman finding each other. It was no mere coincidence. God had brought them together. Ruth and Boaz married and became the great-grandparents of David, the future king of Israel, and from David descended Joseph, who was married to Mary, the mother of Jesus.

God does intervene today and, if we ask him, he can guide us to the best place for us. What we need to do, as Ruth did, is seek God in every situation – to remain selfless, with pure motives and God will honour that.

The social stigma about being single sometimes leads to a pressure to marry and therefore possibly to marry the wrong person simply out of a fear of being permanently single. Marrying the wrong person may, for some, seem better in the short term than remaining single, but in the long term, it could be devastating.

Be brave and wait on the Lord (Psalm 27:14). His purposes for us are perfect. Let us not be fooled into thinking that we know better. For if it is in God's plan for us to find a partner, we can be certain that it will happen in his good time.

Take It Further

Bible Study

1 Corinthians 7:8–39; Ruth 1 and 2.

Talking Points

Marriage and singleness both have advantages and disadvantages. Whichever situation you are in, it is easier to see the advantages of the other. Make a list of all the advantages and disadvantages of each.

How can singles and those married help each other?

For Action

Still at school

Christian work is often hindered by the fact that couples with children can't get out at the same time without having to pay a babysitter, and many single parents are totally tied down. Why not consider setting up a babysitting system, offering to look after children free of charge, for parents who want to take part in church activities? Get an adult to advise you, and go about it in a professional way.

Still single

Invite some other singles round and discuss the possibility of starting a 'singles support group'.

Dating

Organize an outing or a dinner party where you invite some 'unattached' friends. Don't just be interested in, or friends with, other couples.

Chapter 10

Finding the Partner – How Do I Know?

The climbing divorce rate suggests that 'love' can be wrong or blind. How do I know I am in love? How do I know this person will be a permanent partner and friend? There is no easy or simple answer, but the more we know about love and individuals, the more likely we are to meet the right person.

Everyone has ideas of what the 'right' person will be like, what qualities our 'ideal' partner would have. As Christians we've got to be very careful about having 'ideas' of what our partner will be like. Yes, it's important that we know what kind of things we are looking for, but we are so often dictated to by the world. My friend, the poet Stewart Henderson, provides some of the best advice on falling in love:

On Falling in Love
(from *Assembled in Britain*)

Approach it properly
Don't go daft over lipstick
Or the way

93

The body shapes itself in certain places
Refrain from finding your belle
Then imagining her
Bikini-clad with seductive lips
Offering you a Martini
On an isolated beach in the Caribbean.
This is known as fantasy
Which is famous for its short-term attractions
And will cause you to go out
And find another advert.
Fall in love with the person
The skin, the teeth, the hair
Get to know her giggle
The way she holds a cup of coffee
Love without walls.
Approach it properly.

In some sections of society, as long as a man finds a woman and the woman finds a man, everything is OK. As one gets older and more mature, matters become slightly different, for what one considers as 'good looks', for example, are no longer paramount, and other issues and factors become increasingly important. Physical attractiveness is no longer the major decisive factor for love and we need to be looking for qualities that last.

'Finding the right partner' can seem daunting! (And that is an understatement!) When we are dating, we can often feel swayed from one emotion to another – we really like this person, but have no idea whether it could last. At a certain age (I might suggest 21 years upwards), however, dating should become less of a frivolous pastime and the future of a relationship should be seriously assessed. If we are to consider that this could be a partner for life, we need to think seriously.

The question arises – how far should we balance

romance and reason? It seems cold and cynical to only view relationships in terms of a practical conclusion that a long-term commitment would be successful or otherwise. However, the danger is that because the process seems so overwhelming, we tend to focus on our feelings as opposed to common sense. We listen to our fluttering heartbeats, sexual chemistry and hope for a bit of luck.

Ultimately, alongside the many other major choices that we have to make in our lives, finding the right partner is one of the biggest and most important decisions that we will have to make. For this reason, we should prepare ourselves for this decision. We need to know what it is that we are looking for and evaluate our criteria realistically.

Looking at the marriage vows is a good place to start. What are the promises that we would be making?

'For Better For Worse, For Richer For Poorer, In Sickness and In Health . . .'

First, is your partner reliable? Is there a large focus on material possessions, or on pleasure? Do they have an unhealthy interest in earning and spending as much money as possible? Do they drink a lot? Are they someone who will stick by you whatever the circumstances?

Selfishness

Love is self-giving; therefore, being selfish is not only opposite to love, but also against it. It would be quite easy to discern whether one is selfish. Maybe this does not easily surface within a relationship but seeing them within a family setting may be more revealing. Do they insist on their own way? Are they wrapped up in their own feelings and interests? Now of course we all have faults and these need to be pointed out. By God's grace our attitudes need to change, but continued selfish incidents before marriage are not a healthy sign. Being mature means being flexible. Partners who seem to be like little kids, people who are very easily hurt and end up holding grudges, people who freak out and fall to pieces over little things – these are all immaturities. It would be good to see signs of maturity before marriage.

Health

Maybe one partner has a history of psychological, emotional or physical illness. It would be sad if one partner married out of sympathy for the other. The marriage can, of course, be very happy and successful, but will inevitably require and demand incredible patience. The partner needs to be aware of this and if the illness occurs again, possibly with deep depression, remember the vows you make on your wedding day are for better or for worse.

This vow is really requesting that we avoid 'dream' worlds. Life is a combination of joys and sorrows, and marriage is certainly not immune to sorrows. If one partner is ill, the couple must love and adjust. We must be constant in all circumstances.

'Forsaking All Others . . .'

Infidelity

Infidelity is unfaithfulness. When one partner discovers that the other has also been seeing someone else intimately – be warned. If this happens before marriage it could be an indication of continued disloyalty during marriage. There will be a lot of erotic attraction during both courtship and marriage and if there are few signs of faithfulness in this period, then the chances are it may prove to be more of a problem after marriage when the realities of life are less exciting than in the courtship period. If there is to be a profound change, it should happen *before* marriage.

Other Characteristics To Avoid . . .

Spiritual lukewarmness

You may both call yourselves Christians, but one of you now feels fed up with church and therefore rarely attends, prayer is non-existent and any enthusiasm to follow Christ and live by his teaching seems to be out. If this is so before marriage, it may not improve after marriage. A wife or husband hardly enjoys going to church alone. As a consequence, your own commitment to Christ may become diluted. Sharing your faith together can be one of the most rewarding aspects of a married life; living for Jesus together. It is vital to consider this during courtship.

Disagreement about children

If one partner makes it clear that they don't want children and one really desires them – to move into a marriage is no guarantee of a change. A friend of mine married a man who didn't want children, hoping that with time things would change. After several years she did get pregnant. They are now divorced. (I must stress that they did have other problems in their relationship – but the 'no children' issue was always the prominent one.) Now one partner may not articulate it as 'I don't want any children' but may be very impatient or very hard with other family children – this may be a sign and should certainly be worked through before marriage.

Now let's consider the healthy, positive qualities that would be a good sign of having the right partner.

Positive Qualities

Compatibility

It is good if there is some similarity in interests and tastes. This ensures that quality time can be spent in activities that are enjoyed together. For example, if one reads novels while the other reads comics, exchange of reading material will be difficult and sharing will not be very deep. Maybe a rather prominent difference in family background could cause potential problems. The girl brought up with wealth may find moving from an affluent lifestyle to a council flat difficult and trying. We can be very charitable to each other during courtship and therefore ignore barriers and potential problems, but for love's sake, think, talk and pray these things through before marriage. When people enter marriage from very different backgrounds, preparation is essential and the need for adjustment must be thought and worked through. Otherwise too many differences, resulting in too many tensions, could eventually drown out love. Please note: differences aren't wrong and can bring balance into a relationship, but it is essential that the main differences are discussed and prayed through.

Temperament

Temperament means the general attitude or frame of mind. The issue is not whether you as a couple are a blend of likes and opposites, but whether you understand each other's temperament and can adjust to it. Big differences, for example serious versus jovial, mean greater adjustments in marriage. Remember, an accurate reading of your partner's temperament is not seen on 'dates', where one endeavours to be on good behaviour, but an assessment can be made in a relaxed, casual atmosphere with family or close friends.

Partnerships can thrive on opposite characteristics and create complementary and dynamic tensions. But, sometimes, there is a thin line between tensions and the potential to drift apart. Differences that can give energy to one marriage might destroy another.

Attitudes to marital roles

If you are a woman, it is more than likely you will have your own job before marriage. Future roles need to be discussed before making a long-term commitment. A woman who feels she has a definite vocation, yet is married to a man who thinks she should be at home once the children are born, will have a tumultuous marriage. Talk about the roles and, more importantly, find out what the attitude of your partner is to the role of husband or wife.

A Perfect Match?

If you are concerned that you and your partner are not a 'perfect match', then don't worry – there is no such thing.

There comes a time where we have to dispel our ideals and be realistic. Even the seemingly best-suited couple will have gaps and conflicts that they will have to bridge and work through. As with everything in this world, we will never find perfection, but with enough love and commitment these conflicts can be resolved.

Whereas there is no such thing as a 'perfect match', there are plenty of potential 'wrong matches'. I think that we could all think of people that, however hard we tried, would be unlikely to be good partners.

We do not need to find a match that is already perfect, but one that has the potential to be great. Marriage is dynamic – it is a state that is always changing and developing. Therefore, we need someone who has the willingness and commitment to work at being the perfect match, rather than just to remain who they are now. Similarly, we must also be prepared to adapt, be flexible and work at resolving difficulties that might arise.

Some people believe that there is just one person out there for you, like a key that only fits one lock. A successful partnership would therefore depend solely on whether this unique person could be found. This is a myth. You only have to see this in the case of when a wife/husband is widowed; they can marry again and be just as happy with someone completely different. It is dangerous to think that you have to wait for a specific person; it puts all the emphasis on finding the 'right' person before marriage and nothing on 'being' the right person after marriage.

How Do You Know You Are In Love?

At the heart of all our thinking, that is the question, the issue at stake. How do I know that I am marrying the right person?

I faced this issue when I was dating my wife Killy. I asked a friend, Mary Habershon, 'How can I know?' and she said, 'Do you want to spend the rest of your life without Killy?' That was such a helpful question. I knew straight away I wanted to spend my life with Killy. Love will grow or decline, and couples cannot necessarily explain how they know they are in love – but we still need some basis for knowing, particularly when so many films portray dreamy, instant love, with couples living happily ever after. This type of love is not normal practice. May I say this again – *this is not normal practice*!

The more we know about love, the more we know our partner's weaknesses, strengths, joys, sorrows, the more this indicates that a relationship is deep and therefore building for permanency. A future partner should be someone that you can bond with in the four main areas of life. In social settings and with friends; understanding their minds and reasoning; being sexually attracted to one another and being able to share the same spiritual beliefs.

In the book, *Captain Corelli's Mandolin*, this is the advice given by a father to his daughter on the nature of 'real' love:

Love is a temporary madness; it erupts like volcanoes and then subsides. And when it subsides you have to make a decision. You have to work out whether your roots have so entwined together that it is inconceivable that you should ever part. Because this is what love is. Love is not breath-lessness, it is not excitement, it is not the promulgation of promises of eternal passion, it is not the desire to mate every second minute of the day, it is not lying awake at night imagining that he is kissing every cranny of your body. No, don't blush ... I am telling you some truths. That is just being 'in love' which any fool can do. Love itself is what is left over when being 'in love' has burned away, and this is both an art and a fortunate accident.

Your mother and I had it, we had roots that grew together underground, and when all the pretty blossom had fallen from our branches we found that we were one tree and not two. But sometimes the petals fall away and the roots have not entwined. . . . Imagine the desolation. Imagine the imprisonment.

Louis de Bernieres

Love can also be confused with infatuation. Infatuation can be dangerous, as we can be blinded to both wrong and right partners. On the one hand, we can be so overwhelmed with adoration for our partner that we fail to see or recognize their imperfections. Strong sexual desires are normal in a relationship, but can also be misleading in the same sense. Excitement, expectation and passion can temporarily detract from the practical signs that this partnership may not have such strong foundations.

In the same way, there may be a good friend who is very suitable for you as a potential partner. However, you may not feel the warm glowing buzz or same intense feeling of being 'in love' with them. If you valued infatuation, this too could mislead you and distract you away from someone who may make an excellent partner for you.

Take advice. We tend to believe that we always know exactly what is best for us when looking for a partner. But, this is not always the case. Listen to what your friends and family think. Observing you both, they can often see more clearly than you can when you are in the midst of a whirlwind romance.

Take your time – never feel pressurized to make a commitment before you are ready to do so. Allow the relationship time and space to cool down emotionally, so that you can think objectively. Be honest with yourself, and if you do think that there may be potential problems, address them sooner rather than later.

Here are some questions to ask yourself and each other:

1. *Could we live together happily?*
   Are there really too many differences? Have you already seen signs of them bubbling up and exploding? This could ruin any love you think exists. Or, after evaluating your differences, dislikes, likes, background, education, hopes for the future, do you still believe you can live together happily?

2. *Are you really yourself in your partner's company?*
   Or are you trying to look good, be good? Have you relaxed enough to be yourself? A healthy sign would be that you have.

3. *Do you share with each other?*
   Do you share your feelings, your inner self? If so, then this does indicate trust and confidence. This is a good sign of love, as sharing intimately on this level can be painful.

4. *Are you happy simply making your partner happy?*
   If you both are, then that is self-giving love. If not, love will die.

Saying 'yes' to the above questions does not mean you now go and buy a ring and announce your engagement, but your answers to the questions are a signpost. The final confirmation is the Lord's confirmation and *you will know*. Don't worry about how you will know. *You will know*.

Take It Further

Bible Study

Proverbs 31:10ff; Psalm 45; Micah 6:8
Proverbs 31 presents a picture of ideal womanhood. Psalm 45 presents an ideal man. Micah 6:8 is relevant to us all.

Talking Points

What do you think of programmes such as *Blind Date?*

Most of us have a kind of 'ideal image' of a person of the opposite sex. What is your ideal man/woman? What factors have helped to form this ideal? Is it actually realistic?

What should you be looking for in a partner?

For Action

Think about the reasons why people go out with each other – which are valid and which aren't. Write down a list of conditions to be met before you enter a 'steady' relationship with someone.

Dating

Before you take the plunge, think: are you *really* intended for each other? If the answer is 'yes', praise God and pray for your future together. If not, have the courage to part now. If you don't know, don't push it – ease off and just wait. You may need a wise older Christian to advise you. But remember, they can only give you advice, they can't decide for you.

Chapter 11

Loneliness

Loneliness is a universal phenomenon. For some, it may only be a fleeting feeling that visits on dark, gloomy days, but for others it may be far more a reality of life.

Reading Bertrand Russell's autobiography, I was struck by the number of times he spoke of loneliness. Albert Einstein in a letter to a friend wrote, 'It is strange to be known so universally and yet to be so lonely'. Mother Teresa in an interview remarked, 'The greatest disease in the world today is not starvation. The greatest killer is loneliness.'

While TV and radio help to keep us in touch with the world, the daily screen full of busy, exciting, active people is a stark contrast to the humdrum armchair, the TV dinner and a mug of coffee. With so much happening, we feel worse when we are alone.

This feeling can occur at any time in an individual's life. Loneliness affects the young, the elderly, those who live busy lives and those who have plenty of time on their hands. When I visit an old people's home to speak, the faces looking at mine often seem lonely. Some of them must occasionally feel that they don't count, that they are of no significance.

Besides old age, the period of life in which people are most susceptible to loneliness is adolescence. The adolescent needs support as she or he moves towards adulthood. If that support isn't there, loneliness can seem overwhelming.

The sentiment expressed by a girl in Carson McCuller's play *A Member of the Wedding* seems to be a universal experience of adolescence:

> The trouble with me is that for a long time I have been just an 'I' person. All other people can say 'we'. All people belong to a 'we' except me.

Children also experience loneliness. The small girl who doesn't want her parents to go out in the evening dreads being lonely. She may not be able to articulate her feelings, but her tears reveal them vividly. Both married and single adults are susceptible to loneliness. A mother who has raised her family can feel that her job has been done and that she no longer matters.

Loneliness can also occur as a result of losing someone important – either through death or a broken relationship. This can leave us feeling lost and empty and craving the company and intimacy of a special friendship.

Society itself can contribute to loneliness: our consumer society fosters loneliness because of its emphasis on possessions. People are encouraged to judge themselves by the things they own. To judge the value of personal existence by the possessions accumulated is to court loneliness.

If we are hungry, our stomach growls for food and we can think of nothing else until we are satisfied. In the same way, the emptiness we feel when we are lonely is a hunger for others. We are sometimes forced to the extremes to satisfy this hunger. In the film *Castaway*, Tom Hanks played a man who is stranded on a desert island for years. When deprived of people, he creates a pseudo-friend out of a football, which he personalizes and talks to.

The film *Fight Club* depicts the life of Jack who, struggling with loneliness and boredom with life, starts frequenting cancer and disease support groups as a way to meet and bond with others. Professing to be incurably ill and feigning a variety of other ailments, he finds the comfort, sense of belonging and security he longs for through the pity of others. He soon discovers that this intimacy can also be found through violence, and through the Fight Club he finds the respect and friendship he has always longed for. God created people for loving relationships and to need contact with other people, and if we do not receive it we will find ways that are not healthy to fulfil this emptiness.

Loneliness is the feeling of not mattering to anyone, of being insignificant, of being isolated even when surrounded with people. It is a craving of people and social contact – for deeper relationships. It is one of the most disturbing effects of spiritual poverty, and a symptom of our uncaring society.

If you are lonely, try to understand loneliness as deeply and thoroughly as you can. Understanding something is the first step towards handling it, and winning the battle against it. If you are looking for suggestions to put into practice, I would recommend you pay special attention to the following three areas:

Friendship

The experience of being loved is the greatest antidote to loneliness. One of the marvellous things about love is that it focuses on you. The friend always says, at least implicitly, 'I like and love you, because you are you.'

However, friendship doesn't take place until people allow it to take place. Friendship is a loving relationship and all loving relationships are chosen. Friendship, however, demands that each person plays an equal role in the relationship. When the sharing disappears, I think the friendship disappears and the person becomes an acquaintance.

Even the strongest person is quite fragile. We bruise easily. There was a woman who had an 'exclusive' relationship with her husband. Sadly he died. She was left alone and she had no one. The key to solving this woman's problem was for her to come out of herself, to open herself to others, to give and receive. Loneliness tends to enclose us, friendship to open us up. In developing and deepening friendships remember always to be concerned about giving rather than getting, helping rather than being helped. Of course, the paradox of human existence is that the giver often gains more than the receiver.

Activity

If loneliness is a problem, it helps to examine your patterns of activity. Each person has their own lifestyle and some lifestyles may hamper rather than help. Are you on your own too much? Do you have any hobbies? Does your job help or hinder your battle with loneliness? Does your recreation help you to be less lonely?

Be active and engage with as much as possible. Try to direct your energies towards something positive. A weekly visit to the cinema, a discussion group or visits to the sick and aged can redirect your attention and interests and put loneliness into a different perspective. Activity will give us structure and may also create a forum to meet new people with similar interests

Feelings

Recognize the feelings of loneliness. Our feelings tell us about ourselves. They send us messages. There are no unimportant feelings. From them we gain some insight into ourselves. Talk about them, write them down and try to express them. We might be able to see where these feelings are coming from and what they are connected to in our lives. As we begin to see the connections, we will be more in a position to make changes.

Jesus must have been very sensitive to other people's loneliness because he was always giving people a new sense of their importance. He spent his public ministry revealing his Father to people, trying to show them that they are not alone, but that his Father passionately loves them.

Even more than the experience of love between people, the most powerful way to end feelings of loneliness is to experience God's love for us. This was Jesus' basic message: our heavenly Father loves us and wants to share his kingdom with us.

Perhaps the loneliest moment in history was Jesus' experience in the Garden of Gethsemane before his arrest. Remembering that Jesus was a man, we should try to imagine his feelings then as vividly as we can.

Three times Jesus returned to his friends to find them

sleeping. When we need our friends, ask for their help and then are let down, we experience an intense kind of estrangement. The entire experience of the Passion – the cross-examination, the ridicule, the abandonment by his friends, the beatings and the crucifixion – must have intensified Jesus' sense of isolation. Yet by lovingly handing himself into his Father's hands, Jesus survived the loneliness.

As a Christian, ultimately, any loneliness I feel is combated by my love of God and being loved by God. I have found that all other love merely mirrors God's love; all other love is a drop from the infinite ocean of divine love.

In the seventies Al Green sang, 'It's you I want, but it's him [God] I need'. In the nineties, we were told no choice is necessary. Lenny Kravitz on his album *Are You Gonna Go My Way?* mixes sexual licence and God:

> I need you and I need love.
> I need truth and I need God.
> Lay your body next to mine.

We are bombarded with confusing messages. What and who can we trust? People can let us down. Friends disappoint and families can fracture. However, we have the promise of a friend who sticks closer than a brother (Proverbs 24). We have a God who is constant, loving and 'there'.

Jesus Christ is the way, the truth and the life. To trust in Jesus Christ won't solve every problem, but without Jesus Christ, any problem can ultimately be overcome.

The Lord declares: '. . . Those who honour me I will honour.'
1 Samuel 2:30

Take It Further

Bible Study

Psalm 27.

Talking Points

What's the difference between being lonely and being alone?

When did you feel most lonely?

What helpful ways have you found to deal with loneliness?

How can we structure the church to combat loneliness?

For Action

Think of someone you know who might be lonely and do something to help.

Appendix

Notes For Leaders

Listening To Someone Else's Confession

If you are in the position of being asked by someone to receive their confession, make sure you follow these guidelines very carefully:

1. Make sure no one else is within earshot.
2. Make sure that you keep anything that is said to you scrupulously confidential.
3. Don't look shocked or be judgemental or condemning. On the other hand, don't give the impression that sin doesn't matter.
4. Help the other person to pray a prayer of confession. They are confessing to God with you as a witness, not to you.
5. Assure them of God's forgiveness, using 1 John 1:8–9.
6. You may feel that in extreme cases someone needs to take action, e.g. to make restitution, make an apology to someone, or inform the police of a crime. In some situations you may feel they need further specialist help or counselling. Encourage and help them to take whatever steps are necessary.

Other Books by J. John

Look Before You Leap
Preparing for Marriage

We are constantly being told that marriage is a doomed institution. The prevailing attitude is that you can try marriage if you want – just don't expect it to last.

Popular speaker J. John has written *Look Before You leap* because he believes that marriage *does* work and he wants to help make it work for others too.

In *Look Before You Leap* J. John demonstrates the foundations required to build a healthy marriage that will work.

Specifically he covers the following areas:

- What marriage and love are all about.
- Singleness.
- The delicate issues of dating.
- The alternatives to marriage.
- The awesome seriousness of making *that* decision.

Whether engaged or contemplating marriage, this book, with its thoughtful and witty, down-to-earth wisdom, is for all those thinking about getting married.

Till Death Us Do Part
Building and a Sustaining a Healthy Marriage

We are constantly being told that marriage is a doomed institution. The prevailing attitude is that you can try marriage if you want – just don't expect it to last.

Popular speaker J. John believes that marriage *does* work and he wants to help you make it work for you.

In *Till Death Us Do Part* he discusses:

- Creating a marriage: the wedding, the early days, and the principles of making your marriage a success.
- Defending your marriage: resolving conflicts, affair-proofing, crisis management and marriage repair.

Whether you are just married or have been married for years, are happily married or struggling, this book, with its thoughtful and witty, down-to-earth wisdom, is for you.

Walking With God
Searching for Meaning in an Age of Doubt

Living life is like walking along a path: there are choices to be made and obstacles to face. But there are lots of questions.

- How do we find the right way?
- Is there a destination at the end of it all?
- Can anybody help us along the path of life?

Around 2,750 years ago, a prophet spoke to a society that was asking the same questions. 'What does God want?' he asked and – in the next breath – gave the answer: 'To act justly and to love kindness and to walk humbly with your God.'

In this book you will find there are answers. There is a right way to walk through life, there is a destination, and there is someone who will walk along the path of life with us.

The Life
A Portrait of Jesus

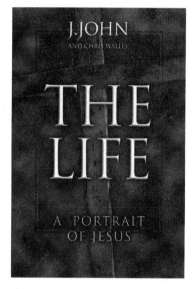

There is no denying the importance of Jesus Christ in the history of humankind.

He has walked through the last two thousand years of history, of empires, governments, political systems and philosophies and has remained as a dominant, challenging, yet mysterious presence.

In *The Life: A Portrait of Jesus* J. John and Chris Walley achieve an uncommon blend – a serious book for popular use and a popular book for serious reading.

If you want to know who Jesus is, then read *The Life* and be rewarded.